TED AND I

TED AND I

A Brother's Memoir

Gerald Hughes

Illustrations by the author

Thomas Dunne Books
St. Martin's Press
New York

THOMAS DUNNE BOOKS.
An imprint of St. Martin's Press.

TED AND I. Copyright © 2012 by Gerald Hughes. All rights reserved.
Printed in the United States of America. For information, address
St. Martin's Press, 175 Fifth Avenue, New York, N.Y. 10010.

www.thomasdunnebooks.com
www.stmartins.com

Library of Congress Cataloging-in-Publication Data

Hughes, Gerald, 1920–
  Ted and I : a brother's memoir / Gerald Hughes ; foreword by
Frieda Hughes.
    p. cm.
  ISBN 978-1-250-04527-0 (hardcover)
  ISBN 978-1-4668-4397-4 (e-book)
  1. Hughes, Ted, 1930–1998—Childhood and youth. 2. Hughes,
Gerald, 1920—Childhood and youth. 3. Poets, English—20th
century—Biography. I. Title.
  PR6058.U348H84 2014
  821'.914—dc23
  [B]

                                          2014026705

St. Martin's Press books may be purchased for educational, business,
or promotional use. For information on bulk purchases, please contact
Macmillan Corporate and Premium Sales Department at 1-800-221-
7945, extension 5442, or write specialmarkets@macmillan.com.

First published in Great Britain by The Robson Press, an imprint of
Biteback Publishing Ltd

First U.S Edition: December 2014

10   9   8   7   6   5   4   3   2   1

To my English and Australian family, my loving wife Joan and our two sons, Ashley and Brendon.

Contents

Acknowledgements

There are a number of people I would particularly like to thank for their encouragement and invaluable help in what has really become a family affair.

My niece Frieda not only suggested that I write the book but has generously contributed a moving and insightful foreword, which I greatly appreciate. Olwyn, my sister, has been a great source of encouragement too, jogging my memory and contributing valuable details from those early childhood days. I'm also extremely grateful to Ted's widow, Carol, for her ready help and suggestions, and for the extra material she has provided.

Both my wife Joan and our son Ashley proved to be invaluable and patient aides as I sorted through old notes, letters and memories – Ashley and his wife Eileen's command of the computer greatly facilitating communication with both my supportive agent, Ros Edwards, and my publisher. If we had had to rely on my handwritten letters to answer their various questions, the book would not have been ready for some time yet!

Thank you also to my friend Graeme Lofts for his advice and encouragement.

Finally, I'm greatly indebted to my publisher, Jeremy Robson, not only for taking my book on, but for his care in helping to develop this memoir throughout the editorial process.

The author and The Robson Press gratefully acknowledge the following sources from which this book has drawn and quoted:

For published poems and letters of Ted Hughes, *Letters of Ted Hughes*, selected and edited by Christopher Reid (Faber and Faber, 2007) and *Ted Hughes Collected Poems*, edited by Paul Keegan (Faber and Faber, 2003), reproduced by kind permission of Carol Hughes and the Estate of Ted Hughes.

All hitherto unpublished material by Ted Hughes reproduced by permission of Carol Hughes and the Ted Hughes Estate.

For letters of Sylvia Plath, reproduced by kind permission of Frieda Hughes and the Estate of Sylvia Plath.

Foreword

My Uncle Gerald, older brother of my father, Ted Hughes, lives near Melbourne in Australia. He has always been an important figure in my life because he was a hugely important figure in the life of my father; we have kept in touch over the years.

Following my father's death in October 1998, Gerald often mentioned to me the letters and phone calls that he was receiving from various individuals wishing to write about my father. He felt obliged to provide answers where he could, and was finding it increasingly tiresome.

I suggested that, instead of remembering the past for others, he should write his own book and remember the past for himself and his family (me included), just as he had once persuaded his mother to write a short memoir of her own for him. And so he has, and here it is.

My father often talked about his family and that

of my mother, Sylvia Plath; he seemed to think it was important that my brother, Nicholas, and I knew something of our origins. I only wish that I remembered more, but children rarely think of asking their older family members about their lives and experiences because they believe there is always tomorrow and that their parents will somehow always be there.

There are reminders of my father's early stories here, however, one of my favourites being about the army pay book that saved his own father's life during a battle in northern France in the First World War. My grandfather kept this pay book in his left pocket over his heart, and when he was hit by shrapnel the pay book took the impact. After the war he kept the tattered remnants of the pay book, still speared with large pieces of shrapnel, together with his sergeant's stripes, his DCM and other medals.

He told me, too, about my Uncle Gerald – his older brother by ten years – who shot rats and rabbits and had taught my father to fish and shoot too. My father also learnt how to cure mole skins, pinning them to the underside of his school desk lid to dry out. (It might have also helped discourage people from borrowing his pencils.) Gerald was something of a natural teacher for my father, just as my father became a natural teacher for my brother and me.

When I was a child my father taught me how to skin

a road-kill badger and cure its pelt, how to shoot, how to cast a fly (we practised on the lawn before putting it into practice on water) and how to draw birds, just as he and his brother had drawn birds together as children.

When my father and his sister, Olwyn, were still very small, their mother, Edith, a great walker and lover of the countryside, took them to all the beauty spots around the Calder Valley when they lived in Mytholmroyd.

My father was around four years old when he started to accompany Gerald on their own explora-tion of the area. Gerald apparently found his little brother to be full of curiosity: he wanted to know the names of the trees, the habitat of birds and breeding patterns of fish. Gerald did all he could to feed this thirst for knowledge, and if there was something he didn't know, he'd look it up in order to inform his little brother. These elements of nature were to become important themes in my father's poetry.

Together, my father and uncle also worked foren-sically and patiently on their toys and inventions. A Chinese proverb that my father often used to quote to me was 'hair by hair you can pluck a tiger bald', a reflection of the patience that he and Gerald applied to the problem-solving and construction tasks they set themselves in their childhood.

After spending the war years working on aeroplanes

in various postings around north Africa such as Algiers and Cairo, enjoying the sun and outdoor life and experiencing all the excitement and tragedy (he had several near-misses of his own) that the RAF had to offer at the time, Gerald became a policeman in Nottingham.

However, after life in the Air Force his new job was something of an anti-climax so, upon seeing an advert in a travel agent's window that promoted migration to Australia, Gerald decided to take the opportunity and move there; he needed a bigger challenge than Nottingham could offer him. He left the UK in 1948, just missing the opportunity to go as a 'ten pound Pom'.

My father was tempted to join Gerald in Australia after he left Cambridge, but in 1956 he met my mother and his priorities changed. Gerald, however, returned to England with his wife Joan on several visits to the family, and my father would take the opportunity to travel around the UK, exploring and fishing with them.

If my father had been able to persuade him, Gerald would have moved into Moortown, the farm in Devon that my father bought with Gerald in mind when I was in my teens. He hoped the farm might tempt Gerald home, but Gerald was too firmly fixed in Australia by this time to consider leaving.

Gerald's great hobbies are painting and golf. He sent my father several of his watercolours over the years, and my father eventually passed them on to me because I liked them so much, but there was little that Gerald could not turn his hand to. On one of his visits, when I was about fifteen, I needed a proper cage for two little zebra finches that I'd bought as pets, so Uncle Gerald made me a little wooden cage with wire mesh, a handle, and top and bottom doors. To me it was the most beautiful little cage in the world, and I was touched that he should spend part of his precious holiday making it for me.

During my 1988 visit to Gerald in Melbourne for Christmas Gerald and I would go out painting together. That was when he introduced me to the artist David Rankin, who later sold several of my etchings through his Port Jackson Press, in Brunswick Street, Fitzroy.

Prints for many leading Australian artists were produced in this studio, and once a week Gerald would go to work in the space that David had set up for him. Propelled by David's enthusiasm he seemed inspired. Paintings later gave way to etchings, which Port Jackson Press sold for him.

My father had met David first when he'd gone over to Australia to read his poetry at the Adelaide Festival in 1976; David subsequently lived in the UK for two years, and so he knew all about Gerald and Gerald's interest in art from my father. It was 1983, when David returned to Melbourne from the UK, that he and Gerald finally got together.

It was easy for me to see why Gerald might have fallen in love with Australia: the vast landscapes with peeling paper bark eucalyptus, the rolling mountains, the strange prehistoric-looking vegetation, the way the sun, so bright in the daytime, drew long shadows in the late afternoon as the colours intensified in the last of the daylight.

The wonderful landscape around the Arapiles at Natimuk, Victoria.

During my visit I fell in love with Australia myself, and in 1991 I became an Australian resident and moved to Perth, Western Australia.

But in April 1997 I got the devastating news that my father was seriously ill and in hospital with cancer. I arrived in the UK on 25 April, stayed two weeks and only returned to Australia to pack up my home and make all the necessary arrangements to return to the UK that July; I wanted to be on the same land-mass as my father and spend more time with him. He died on 28 October 1998 aged sixty-eight.

The last time Uncle Gerald came to England was May 1999, when he and Joan stayed with his sister, my Aunt Olwyn, for my father's memorial service at Westminster Abbey, and then with me at my home in London.

Gerald had encouraged my father's appreciation and knowledge of the countryside, and in turn my father encouraged my brother and me. When my brother died on 16 March 2009 at the age of forty-seven, the countryside and fishing had been a major part of his life; he was an evolutionary ecologist and a professor in the School of Fisheries and Ocean Science at the University of Alaska Fairbanks, conducting research both in Alaska and New Zealand. As for me, the natural world is the basis for much of my writing and painting.

My father's love for his brother ensured that Gerald was part of my life as I grew up, despite the separating miles, and Gerald's love for my father has resulted in this moving tribute, which is a joy for me to read.

Frieda Hughes

Preface

It was only in 2007, when I was eighty-seven, that I
realised unless I began recording particular memories of the childhood years I enjoyed with my brother
Ted and my sister Olwyn – and some of the experiences we shared in later years – they would be lost. So
I embarked on these recollections, which are by no
means a complete record but, I hope, a readable one.

I was particularly encouraged by a line in one of
Ted's letters to me in Australia, where I have lived
since early 1949. 'Wish you could remember more
stories about me – us – when I was small,' Ted wrote.
Well, in these pages I have tried to do just that, and
I am fortunate to have had my sister Olwyn's own
memories to draw on and check things against, as well
as a memoir my mother left. Also, of course, Ted's
poems and the many letters he sent me over the years,
as well as letters and cards we received from Sylvia
Plath – from America, and then from the house they
bought together in Devon.

Those early days in Yorkshire are a special treasure and oh, how we wish we had done this or that differently, as we look back and reflect on time wasted with non-essentials, when it should and could have been spent with loved ones. Clearly we have lost part of ourselves that will never return. This memoir, therefore, is a best personal effort to take hold of a few of the past's memorable moments, when we were joined with it, and part of it, and knew it, and my way of touching it, however briefly, before it, too, is lost.

My on-the-spot sketch of Banksfields, Mytholmroyd, where Ted and I used to go shooting in the late 1930s.

Part I

Childhood

The schoolboy Ted, aged ten.

Chapter One

Hebden Bridge

My earliest memory of life in Hebden Bridge – the charming, old medieval Yorkshire town where I was born – was finding my father's sergeant stripes in a drawer. I must have been around two years old. I remember kneeling on the sitting room floor gazing at the stripes, wondering what they were and being fascinated by them. They became my special treasure. Later I was shown Dad's Distinguished Conduct Medal and the other medals from his war service with the 5th Lancashire Fusiliers in Gallipoli and France, together with his shrapnel-pierced pay book, which created for me a glimpse of the strange and dangerous world I had entered. Dad had been one of only seventeen men from his company to return from Gallipoli, and his medal was awarded for exceptional bravery.

My father, William Henry Hughes (Billy), was born at 4 King Street, Mytholm, Yorkshire, on 15 February 1894. A fit and energetic man, Dad was a skilled wood-working joiner who loved his work with F. & H. Sutcliffe in Hebden Bridge. He was always fully employed – even through the depression that was to come in the 1930s. Dad was good at everything he did, really. I never recall him being ill or taking a day off work. He loved to read the Belgian detective writer Georges Simenon and to listen to records by the fine Irish tenor John McCormack, mostly opera arias. He was also interested in politics, which he used to discuss with his friends in the pub over a pint.

My father's father, Jack – my grandfather – was of Irish extraction and had died young of tuberculosis, leaving his wife Polly to bring up her three children alone – my father, the youngest, John and Mary Alice. Uncle John, a quiet, steady man, and his wife Hilda lived nearby in Mytholm. Mary Alice lived in Manchester with her husband and family and we saw little of them. There seems to have been no extended family in close proximity for either of my paternal grandparents, although Polly used to speak of army forebears, one of whom, a Major Major (Major was Polly's maiden name!), had been born on the Rock of Gibraltar and later served there.

We never knew a great deal about Grandfather Jack, except for his Irish roots and that at the time of his marriage to Polly he lived locally in Crag Vale and was known as Crag Jack. He was equally friendly with the Catholic priest and Protestant vicar, both of whom visited him in his final illness. He seems to have been a pleasant man who liked company and was a great singer. I regret that we children were not more curious and never pressed Polly about her background.

My mother, Edith Farrar, born 18 September 1898, married my father after his return from the First World War. Their first home was a cottage at 2 Oakville Road, Charlestown, Hebden Bridge. I was born on 7 September 1920 at Granny Farrar's house in Foster Lane, also in Hebden Bridge. My mother returned to her own home after a short recovery period. In a memoir she wrote later, and which I came across again only recently, she says that their cottage had only two bedrooms, a living room and kitchen, with an outside toilet, that they paid two shillings and ninepence per week rent and were very happy there. (In the currency of those days, there were twenty shillings in a pound and twelve pence in a shilling.) Her own mother had had eight children, two of whom died in infancy and one, mother's much-loved sister Miriam, as a young woman – all from illnesses that could now be cured.

Mother was a proficient clothing machinist with Dewhirsts in Hebden Bridge. She had taken night-school courses in hat making and always made her own hats, as well as most of her clothes. She had also begun driving lessons, but these were stopped by her father. In her factory she was voted prettiest girl, but only, apparently, when she wore her favourite pink blouse.

Later, when I could walk, Mam would take me down to Granny Hughes's home at 4 King Street, Mytholm. It was a small stone house at the end of a low row of similar cottages, since bulldozed away, which were built in the early nineteenth century to house the labour force required by the large nearby iron and steel foundry.

Granny's house was always bright and spotless, with an array of brass fire tongs and the like in her fireplace, which glowed with the light of winter coal fires. Beyond the sitting room was the stone-flagged kitchen, and this opened onto a long yard with a patch of huge sunflowers, which bloomed every summer, at the end.

Granny had modified the front of her sitting room into a shop with brass weighing scales on the counter. She managed her shop with great efficiency. I well remember her snow-white hair, her white lace blouse and her twinkling blue eyes. Imagine a small boy being left there in her care – in a sweet shop, of all places!

I passed much of the time I spent at Granny's cutting out figures from the stiff white cards that acted as dividers in the boxes of chocolates, of which I had an endless supply. I would pencil in the outline of horses, guns, aeroplanes etc., and then carefully cut them out and colour them in with crayon. This was the beginning of my lifelong interest in sketching and painting.

Each evening, after work, my mother would call for me and off we would go, back to our house. When Dad came with Mam he would carry me most of the way on his shoulders, warning me of the odd bat flying around, particularly if it was dark. 'Watch out for bats!' he would shout.

When I was a little older – around five or six – Dad, who was a keen footballer, would take me up the hill behind our house, through a lovely wooded area to a cleared spot we called The Delph, where he would teach me some of the tricks of good ball control. Dad played centre-half for Hebden Bridge, who were gold medallist football champions before the Second World War. A large northern club wanted to recruit him, but he decided his job was more secure (and better paid!). Mam writes wryly about his footballing days in her memoir: 'I didn't like Billy going off footballing. He would stay out until eleven or twelve o'clock when they played away.'

The hills and woods around Hebden Bridge were a favourite area where my pals and I would play Cowboys and Indians with bows and arrows and toy six-shooters, firing off caps, as the little pink round charges were called – all make-believe, but marvellous fun.

Nearby was a disused quarry with some rusty equipment still in place – a dangerous spot for children, but we played there all the same. One day I remember sliding down a sharp slope and colliding with corroded machinery, severely cutting my left eyebrow. I was on the way home, clutching a blood-soaked handkerchief, when a neighbour stopped me and examined the wound. 'If it had been half an inch lower, young man,' he said, 'it would have got that eye, but it's only the sort of cut boxers get.' This cheered me considerably and the cut was subsequently stitched up by the local doctor.

By this time, I had been attending Mytholm School – not far from Granny's shop – for two years. I don't remember much about my brief time at this school, except that the teachers were warm and friendly and I enjoyed being there.

My father had gone to this same council school in his youth, and he recounted an occasion when the teacher was ringing the school hand bell signalling the end of playtime and it slipped from her hand, tumbling towards my father, who – footballer that he was – instinctively kicked it right over the school wall and across the street. He apologised, but received a light caning.

Otherwise, my father seems to have been a good pupil on the whole, and was something of a star at English grammar. He also remembered, good humouredly, his humiliation when Granny – who had very little money after her husband's early death

– worked as a cleaner and he had to go to school for a time in ladies' boots, a gift from the woman she worked for.

In the 1920s and 1930s, preparations for the annual celebrations of Guy Fawkes Day were a firm ritual in the village during the weeks preceding 5 November and, when I was a little older, my father would bring home a selection of fireworks: a few pinwheels and fountains and two or three rockets. Also some sparklers to be hand held, always a big thrill. All the fireworks in the neighbourhood were let off only after dark, for maximum effect. They were set up on top of the five-foot dry stone wall across the narrow street. We didn't have a bonfire in the village, but I remember seeing large bonfires here and there across the Hebden Valley.

On 5 December 1927, when I was seven, my parents moved to a three-bedroomed end-of-terrace house at 1 Aspinall Street, Mytholmroyd, about a half-hour's bus journey from Charlestown. I was allocated the attic, which gave me plenty of space for my bed and a table, on which I assembled my balsa-wood aircraft. The attic had a skylight, from which I could view the whole of Mytholmroyd township, including St Michael's Anglican church tower and clock. From behind, the grim cliff face of Scout Rock dominated the village, and between our new home and the Rock lay the Rochdale Canal – only a hundred yards from our back door. This skylight view of the town and the mysterious bulk of the Rock and its surrounding hills filled me with excitement as I contemplated the prospect of the adventures now possible in my new kingdom.

A hundred yards further down, the Midgley Road ran from the canal bridge to Burnley Road on the valley floor, leading to Hebden Bridge on the right, with Halifax on the left. Buses and trams provided an excellent service along that road, which was lined on both sides with village shops. Horace Dunkley's the tailor was next to Fisher's fish and chip shop, then there was a cake shop, which sold the most delicious vanilla slices.

Beyond the main road ran the river Calder, which was approximately sixty yards wide and quite deep in places. On the other side of the bridge and on the left was the Anglican church with its extensive cemetery, and beyond that a few houses and sundry shops for a further five hundred yards, leading to the railway and station.

Moving to Mytholmroyd brought us into closer contact with my mother's family. My maternal grandmother, Annie, and her youngest daughter, Hilda, shared a house nearby. Hilda, dark and attractive, worked as secretary to her brothers Tom and Walter, at the successful clothing company the two owned. Tom was married to Ivy Greenwood and they had one son, David, born in 1930, who later ran the brothers' factory for many years. Walter, a big man, around six feet tall, had a warm, generous personality with a lively sense of humour. He married Alice, the best potato pie maker in Yorkshire. They had three children – Barbara, Edwin and James.

Before the First World War, Tom, a keen rose gardener, had attended a business college in Manchester. Whether it was part of the university I'm not sure, but on the strength of his education he was made an officer. Both he and his brother Walter served in the infantry during the war – Tom with the Royal Engineers, Walter with the King's Royal Rifles. Tom was caught in a gas attack, which badly affected his health, and Walter had lain wounded in no-man's land for two days, being shot at by a German sniper the whole time, until rescued by his comrades. Walter used to recall that, as he lay unconscious on the battlefield, in his head he was roaming the hills and valleys around his home, as he had done as a boy. After lengthy hospital treatment he was discharged from the army.

Both brothers suffered from their wounds for the remainder of their lives but, against all odds, they built a solid business in the clothing trade. When Ted went up to Cambridge Tom gave him his leather officers' greatcoat, still in good condition. It was before its time as a fashion but kept Ted warm against the freezing Cambridge winters.

Tom and Walter's younger brother Albert was not

involved with the clothing factory, but pursued a trade as a skilled joiner and cabinet maker. He was married with one daughter, Glenys. His wife Minnie always made us children welcome in their home.

Albert was a keen reader of the popular American author Zane Grey and a lover of that romantic period of American history Grey wrote about in his novels, when the West was won. Under my uncle's influence, I read every Zane Grey book I could lay my hands on. Albert was a great storyteller, with a fine sense of humour. He was a fit, strong man with the physique of a weightlifter. He was also – as were his two older brothers – very handsome.

Uncle Tom, always the scholar, spent many years tracing the history of the Farrar family and got back as far as Guillaume de Ferriere, Master of Horse for William the Conqueror. The name of our French ancestor is as I remembered it. He was not a Norman, but a man from Burgundy. His coat of arms was three horseshoes on a blue bend. Tom's research, which always fascinated us as children, was continued by his son David.

So, with the move to Mytholmroyd, my life was enhanced greatly by the warmth and the intelligence to be found in Mam's family.

It didn't take me long to check out my new neighbourhood, with the canal being quickly investigated.

It was swarming with little fish, mainly gudgeons and sticklebacks, which lived in the deep cracks between the stone blocks lining the canal bank. Later on I discovered that there were also trout to be found, and there was rumour of the occasional pike.

At that time, the canal was being used by horse-drawn barges, which transported goods to the many mills along its banks – from Manchester through to Halifax and beyond – as they had done for two hundred years or more. I noticed that the stone corners of every bridge along the canal were deeply grooved by the friction of barge tow ropes. These barges were generally crewed by a family – father or teenage son at the tiller, wife and children in brightly coloured dresses and hats, all of whom would wave to us as we watched from the bridge or canal bank, always careful to keep our fishing gear and ourselves well clear of the horse and tow rope. The horse would plod steadily ahead with commands from the skipper.

In January 1928 I was enrolled in the Burnley Road Council School, which was only a short distance from our home. I settled in easily and made friends who remained close throughout my life. The headmaster was Mr A. Jackson, whose lectures I still remember well. One such, on the dangers of alcohol, made a lasting – and beneficial – impression on me.

At around this time I also worked as a newspaper

delivery boy with four or five other lads of similar age. We paper boys would arrive early each morning at Mr Tetlow's newsagent's shop in Burnley Road, Mytholmroyd, and there pick up our bags of papers – all correctly marked up by a smiling Mr Tetlow. We delivered those papers – come rain, hail or shine – and received about seven shillings and sixpence per week. We finished our round in time to return home for breakfast and get off to school. All this kept us very fit indeed.

On 26 August 1928 my sister Olwyn was born. She was beautiful and naturally became the centre of attention – bringing me new responsibilities. Olwyn was born in Granny Farrar's new house in Albert Street – only a hundred yards away from our home in Aspinall Street. Since we were surrounded by relatives living in and around the village, many callers suddenly intruded on my previously tranquil life, and I found myself opening our front door frequently to visitors who had come to see the new baby. The family interest had now certainly shifted to Olwyn, but I found satisfaction in being able to help my mother in many ways, and it was an opportunity to renew my relationship with my several uncles and aunties and their families.

Mother's younger sister, Hilda, was a frequent caller. In her memoir, my mother writes:

Hilda used to nurse her [Olwyn] in the evening, putting a little shawl over her head. It was a lovely sunny day when she was born. Mrs Gibson and Mrs Barker [neighbours] loved her, and later I remember her sitting at Mrs Gibson's kitchen table with a little rolling pin, her face smudged with flour, and putting her cakes in tins.

Then, on Sunday 17 August 1930, my brother Ted was born at home at 1.00 a.m. Mother's memoirs state that a bright star was shining through the window of the bedroom where he was born. 'He was a lovely, plump baby,' she writes, 'and I felt very proud of him.' She goes on: 'Sunday was a wet day. Olwyn just could not understand the newcomer ... she cried a lot and finally Mrs Barker took her. Gerald was a darling, practically looked after me and Olwyn.'

I'd like to think this was indeed so, but I'm afraid I can't claim to remember that it was!

Mam was soon up and about again. We used one pram to take Ted and Olwyn for walks around the town and to visit the nearby recreation ground, with children busily enjoying the slide and swings. Olwyn was small and dainty with fair curls; Ted had dark hair 'with lovely blue eyes', as Mother fondly recalls, though the colours of both were to change – his eyes becoming hazel and his hair a mousy colour. As he got older Ted's hair was very fine and floaty and needed hair cream, which gave the impression of darker hair. Mother used to read Wordsworth and had a great love of the countryside. She introduced us all to it with these long walks. We sometimes ended our walks with visits to Uncle Albert and Aunt Minnie, then along to Granny Farrar's – who always had a large tin of assorted sweets to sample.

The Mytholmroyd memorial plaque to Ted by the Canal Bridge on Burnley Road.

In 1932, with my sister enrolled in the Burnley Road School, I spent more time roaming the hills and moors with my pals. I purchased a BSA air rifle for a few shillings and would spend hours hunting around a few of the farms. I obtained permission from the farmers to shoot on their land. On still, early mornings, two or three times a week, I would patiently wait and pick off the odd rat. This was exciting sport for me at the time. What's more, there were rewards, as the farmers were grateful and I was generally given a few eggs. I was already an early riser from my days doing the paper round and, after finishing my morning 'hunt', as I called it, I would cycle off to school.

It was about then too that I discovered adventure magazines such as *Boys' Own*, *The Skipper*, *Rover* and others, selling at twopence per copy. My mother didn't like these magazines, saying, 'There is much better literature available, and I wish you would stop reading them.' She would throw any copies she found into the rubbish bin, but I would retrieve them, leaving one or two unwanted copies in their place, and continue to read and swap with my friends. Eventually Mother won out as my interests changed.

Chapter Two

Early Days

It wasn't long before my brother Ted was running around the house, busy with his toys – particularly with a Hornby clockwork train set that our father had bought us for Christmas. This was set up in the sitting room in front of the fireplace, alongside our upright piano, which stood against the wall, facing the window. I recall one hair-raising occasion when Ted, who would have been about three years old at the time, was loading the little wagons with lead soldiers. Then, just as I was about to start the engine, he reached over suddenly, tripped on the fireside fender and fell into the fire. I immediately jumped up, seized him and lifted him bodily out of the fireplace. He didn't cry much, as I remember, although both his hands were blistered.

The local doctor treated Ted's burns for about three or four weeks, during which time both his arms were bandaged up to the elbows. He never complained, and after the bandages were changed the second or third time, all was healed up, leaving no permanent scarring. He was not affected by all of this and in subsequent years, when we had many camp fires, he showed no fear of them. However, he was careful and always aware. As he once remarked, 'Fires can get up and bite you.'

Granny Farrar had been ill on and off for the past few years with angina. Ted, Olwyn and I would visit her from time to time and try to comfort her – doing little errands etc. She would often ask us to read poetry to her. She particularly liked to hear works by Edward Thomas, the First World War poet who wrote so beautifully about the English countryside. Granny sadly passed away in 1934. Ted was four at the time, Olwyn six.

Granny Farrar was greatly missed. She was a larger-than-life figure who, coming as she did from a farm on 'the tops', still spoke 'the language', as some old man once admiringly said. I remember, as does my sister Olwyn, that she called cushions 'wishins' – a term Olwyn later encountered in her Anglo-Saxon studies at university. We both recall eating the marvellous oatcakes that Granny Farrar used to hang to dry and harden on a wooden-railed clothes-drying contraption she had in her kitchen (rope hitched to the ceiling). We all enjoyed those cakes, spread with lots of butter.

When she was younger, Granny had been a star at

the Hebden Bridge Chapel and gave some wonderful performances at their concerts, singing a song in her powerful voice (farmers always spoke loudly – from working in wide fields in windy weather) about her bicycle, a penny-farthing, which she wheeled onstage. Her singing always embarrassed my mother, who was a quieter, gentler speaker. In her memoir, Mam describes how Annie, stout and handsome with great vitality, could both weep and laugh easily. When she went to the local Wesleyan Chapel and the sermon or hymns touched her, tears would roll down her cheeks under the veil she wore with her best hat.

My Grandfather Farrar had died of asthma when he was sixty years of age. I dimly remember him making me a small, four-wheeled, sit-on wooden horse, which I named 'Jinney' – how I loved that little horse. My mother writes warmly of him in her memoir, saying, 'My father was a power loom tacker – tall with black hair and a rather heavy black moustache. He was quiet, fond of reading and played the violin a little. Also, he was good at mending watches, for which he had infinite patience. He came from a good old local family who were proud of their ancestry.' My grandparents got on peaceably and both worked hard. In the course of their years, they lost three children.

Ted and I both attended Burnley Road Council Primary School, but early in 1932 I changed schools and moved to Hebden Bridge Central School where there were some fine teachers. The headmaster was Mr Glue; the English mistress was Miss Baxter, a Scottish lady; and there was Mr Uttley, who we called 'The Cat' because he never missed any misbehaviour in class.

I enjoyed my time there. Leaving school at fourteen, I began work at my uncle's clothing factory, not far from our home in Banksfields. I also began night-school classes in Hebden Bridge, studying tailors' cutting for the next three years and obtaining a qualifying certificate each year. The plan seemed to be that I would eventually have a managerial role in the factory. I also took woodworking classes – due to Dad's influence. This early training has been of great value to me.

Ted's first camping trip with me was in July 1935 and the weather was good. He was almost five. I told Mam that he wouldn't be far away and that we would camp by the stream at Foster Clough, a narrow strip of virgin woodland about sixty yards wide in places which was a hundred yards beyond Throstle Bower, an area with which Mam was familiar. I remember she said that I must take care as we were so close to the stream: 'You know Ted likes playing in water, making little dams, and floating bits of wood, so don't take his model boat, or he will get wet for sure, and catch cold.'

I promised to keep him dry and safe, and Mam checked our food supplies and rain gear 'just in case'. I didn't own a camera – my first Box Brownie being still in the future – but the details of that first camp with Ted are as clear in my mind as any record on film could be.

I remember Ted's pals came around before we departed – his two inseparable friends Derek Robertshaw and Brian Seymour, and young Donald Crossley – all full of advice for Ted. We packed and were on our way by early afternoon. Ted carried a small bag, and we walked up Midgley Road, past the recreation ground and Uncle Walter's factory, pausing to buy sweets at the small shop further up the road on the left-hand side. There was a large tree in the bottom corner of the field near the stream where we boys would leave messages to our pals. Passing the message tree, we walked up the side of the field along the wire fence that kept cattle out of the clough. Cows would press against that fence in an endeavour to reach the stream, and on that memorable day there were about twenty milling around the fence bordering our camping spot, which was about the only flat area in the whole clough.

We climbed through the wire and erected our Bukta tent, then made a fire and put on the billycan. I remember the long row of very interested cows at the fence, watching every move we made. This didn't appear to worry Ted much, except that they were noisy for a long time before dispersing in the field and settling down. We were quite comfortable and chatted away a while.

It must have been nearly midnight when I was awakened by my father's call, 'Gerald, Gerald', as he came up to the tent. Dad explained that Mam had become very anxious about Ted and that he was taking him back home. I told Dad we were OK, and that the cows were no problem. Dad replied, 'Yes, Gerald, cows are all right, but there was a big bull at the fence when I came up, so Ted comes home, my lad.' I spent the rest of the night on my own, then packed up and left the following day. The mob of cows was just too restless with the bull in their midst.

So ended Ted's very first camping trip. When I arrived home, Mam said that Ted had talked non-stop about the big bull and the cows and how he wanted to go back there again, but that I really must be more careful in future as he was only a little boy.

However, Ted was growing fast and would soon join me on my hunting trips over the hills and around the old farms. He enjoyed the early mornings and was up and ready to go regardless of how early it was or how cold the weather. In winter, he was always care- fully and warmly dressed. He would trot along with me, very nimble and quite silent, pretending to be a Red Indian hunter, absorbing everything. I gave him snippets of information from my little store of knowledge as we walked, such as 'That's a magpie; they are egg stealers'.

On these morning hunting walks Ted and I took to walking backwards up one particular hill to strengthen our leg muscles. We found that looking back down the hill and across the valley gave us a rare thrill – nothing stirring down there and all up here on the hills silent and damp with dew, the morning mist still clinging to the trees.

All the dry stone walls surrounding the high fields were of bare, dark, irregular hand-shaped stones, often covered in moss, and they bordered the Heights Road from the adjacent field one side and the higher bleak moorland on the other. In winter, the snow fell first on the Heights. When it retreated from the valley floor, the snow still hung on up on Hill Brink and the 'Skip Inn' area of the moor's edge, as well as along the Heights Road.

One morning out hunting I remember the temperature dropped well below freezing and, taking aim at a rabbit with my .22 Winchester rifle, the firing pin was so sluggish it barely fired the cartridge until I had wiped it clean of all oil. Being up there was like flying. We knew that we had to return to the valley for work and school and all the doings of the day, but we would put off the return journey, heading homewards only when the sun was up warming the hillside. As we reached the lower fields, we would be greeted by the chorus of cock-crowing from the hen pens along the top of Banksfields, with the accompaniment of steam trains across the valley beyond the river Calder, huffing and puffing as the engine wheels spun for traction on icy lines.

At night, Ted and I would open the attic window and, particularly when snow lay in the valley, we would listen to the trains shunting trucks and how the engine strained and pushed. The wheels would spin and puff to a standstill before having another try at moving the frozen trucks. These memories Ted later wrote about with nostalgia.

On other days, from our old campsite on Broadbottom Field, we would carefully hunt around Hill House Farm, going on to Redacre Wood, where we would watch squirrels, then up through the wood to Clough Hole and so on up the creek to Hill Brink, which we renamed, unofficially, Sugar Loaf, as it was snow capped in winter, from where we could often shoot a rabbit or wood pigeon. This was also the hill from which Ted and I and our pals flew our gliders. The steady breezes coming up the valley were perfect for spectacular flights, and also for flying kites.

On the way home, we would go into Redacre Wood, where Ted had a tom-tom drum hidden, and we'd sit and drum away for a while. Occasionally, we would go along past the gasometer and through into the wood, cutting up to the Ancient Briton gravesite through to the higher arm of the wood and up to Hill House Farm. We'd often stop at Royd Ices – situated at the immediate entrance to Redacre – and oh how good that delicious chunk of ice cream tasted, wrapped in greaseproof paper! Royd Ices were favourites in the village. Throughout the warmer months they sold their wares from a couple of horse-drawn carts, that ice cream bell such a welcome sound. Olwyn and Mother also enjoyed a wafer or cornet. Royd Ices used large quantities of fresh eggs in their ice cream and we would help clean up the high piles of egg shells. A pile of shells meant free ice cream for us!

Ted was fascinated by all wildlife – hawks and owls in particular. We never shot any of these birds – only farm rats, wood pigeons, rabbits and a couple of stoats up on the edge of the moor, together with the odd grouse.

On occasion, when we had a spare rabbit, and if it was not too early, we would call on Old McKinley, a retired gamekeeper, and his wife, who lived above Hill House Farm in a pleasant, long, low, white-stone bungalow. McKinley would occasionally walk with us along the lane above his cottage, recounting interest-ing stories of his life as a gamekeeper on some large shooting estate down south. I remember he still wore his old keeper's hat and official jacket with its large pockets and brass buttons – each button embossed with the coat of arms of the titled family who had employed him. Ted and I were entranced by his stories. Little did we realise that he was one of the last of the old-style keepers, wearing his keeper's clothing and hat like a uniform and faithful to his calling to the end.

Frequently when we were out and it rained we would find shelter in a barn or shed, of which there were many on the old farms where we walked. One day we sheltered in a long-disused hen house and set up a small stone as a target on the end wall. Ted was developing into a fine shot and we took turns shooting with the .177 BSA air rifle. Ted fired, and then cried out in pain and clutched his face. I quickly examined him and found that the rifle slug had ricocheted back and embedded itself in his forehead, right between his eyes, and had then dropped out. I stemmed the blood, which was not much, and applied antiseptic the moment we returned home. We decided not to tell our parents and we luckily got away with it. Throughout all our many shooting trips, this was the only accident, as we'd been taught to handle guns with great care. However, I still feel a chill whenever I remember that near-disastrous incident.

Our last target competition took place many years later, in Devon in the 1970s, on Ted's farm, Moortown, when we shot at a four-inch page from Ted's notebook – five shots each, standing at eighty yards. Only three of my shots hit the target, but Ted's were grouped in a three-inch circle – extremely fine shooting at that range. I still have the target from that last encounter.

But back to 1935... My father made a rabbit hutch and erected it on our five-yard strip of garden, just bordering the pavement. Those tiny gardens actually cut into the road – illegally, I'm sure – but traffic was very light and no one objected. We bought black-and-white rabbits, which were given to Ted to look after. He also kept two white mice for a time and would carry one around in his pocket. On one occasion he put the mouse down the back of our cousin Glenys's dress! Poor Glenys shrieked with ticklish laughter and vigorously wriggled until the startled mouse dropped out. She made Ted vow never to do it again. He also lost one mouse in my attic while watching me build a model plane one day. We searched everywhere without success. However, a few days later I found the mouse in my bed. It must have lived on the biscuit Ted left out on the floor with water in a tin lid. I remember him saying, 'That mouse must have crawled out of your bed, then back again; what a clever little mouse he is.'

By 1936, when Ted was six years old, he came with me wherever I went, asking endless questions. I explained all that went on in the hills and farms above our home, and told him about the plentiful wildlife. We could see hawks, magpies, rooks, jackdaws, wood

pigeons, partridge and grouse – as well as a multitude
of smaller birds. There were the odd squirrel and fox,
and higher up, on the moor's edge, stoats and weasels.
So Ted was steadily absorbing the fascinating life of
the countryside, and what a wonderfully retentive
memory he had, as we saw later in his poems – and
what a faithful little companion for me he was on all
these expeditions over the hills and moors.

Olwyn never accompanied us on our days roaming
the hills, but was at home or with her friends doing
other things. She always seemed busy and enjoying
life. Sometimes she made forays into the surrounding countryside with family groups or her own young
friends, picnicking, swimming in the rocky Crag Vale
mountain pool, enjoying the Brownies occasionally
or playing with Ted while I was at school or out with
my friends.

In later years Ted and I often recalled those early
days with all our happy memories. He thought, as
I still think, that Redacre Wood was a special place
where one stepped back in time. I remember vividly
the high, oak-studded slope of the wood; the peace
of the place. We never experienced such a wonderful bird chorus anywhere else as that heard along the
bottom path through the wood. Ted once said, 'I love
the wood and hope no one ever builds on it. What a
dull old world it would be without wildlife.' He was
so right.

Redacre Wood still exists intact as I remember it in the 1930s. Some years ago it was ravaged by fire, but Ted's old school pal Donald Crossley assured me that it has returned to its original condition. Some of the old trees we climbed are no longer there, of course, but the wood is still a magical place and birds still sing, and all seems to be as it was in our childhood there – right down to the masses of bluebells.

Redacre Wood, where we camped and climbed trees.

It was about this time that an RAF bomber circled the valley in thick fog above Mytholmroyd. I can still remember the heavy drone of those engines up and down the valley, then the crash as the plane flew into a nearby hill on the edge of the moor near Midgley, followed by silence. I believe there were survivors, but the crash site was cordoned off for days while the

RAF collected the wreckage. Finally, they went away, leaving lots of interesting bits and pieces of the plane behind. Ted and I immediately salvaged a few useable pieces of light tubing from which we made a model plane to fly over the same hills.

A local man advised us that the crash site was almost on top of a WWI rifle range and he showed us where the actual targets were placed. We knew there must be thousands of bullets embedded there, and so they proved to be. We dug up large quantities of them and, back in our kitchen and unbeknownst to Mam, placed them in a shallow tin lid on our gas oven top. The lead contents melted out into blobs, which we flattened, shaped and used on the keels of our model sailing boats. We kept the process a secret, fearing Dad would stop us doing it. We knew nothing about explosive bullets – we just assumed the ones we had found were old and dead. Fortunately, there were no disasters and we finished melting the bullets in two or three days. We didn't repeat the exercise, which was just as well, considering the toxic effects of lead!

Up in the attic there was always some model plane or kite or boat under construction. Ted and I set up a work table near the skylight to get the full benefit of that single window. A local pal, Harry Sykes, suggested we build one each of the same model plane and see whose flew best. Our model had the largest wing span

I had ever built, being two-and-a-half feet wide and propelled by rubber bands, which gave enough power to get the plane airborne up to twenty or thirty feet. Ted readily helped in the building operation, which took weeks to finish. It looked good, as did Harry's, but neither craft flew well. Our simple balsa-sheet winged gliders were much better fliers. Ted often said, 'Let's take the glider up to Sugar Loaf; we get great flights up there.' And we did. A happy time – all too brief – for both of us.

When not exploring the hills, we would often find ourselves drawn to the river Calder, which flowed alongside the main road the length of Mytholmroyd. The river, with its fascinating debris, was an ever-changing source of interest to us. There were always lots of tin cans caught up on the pebbled high spots, which we refloated and then did our best to sink with well-aimed small stones before the fast-flowing river swept them away around the next bend. The bed of the Calder as it flows through Mytholmroyd is 90 per cent pebbles of all sizes, but most about the size of a medium potato – the perfect size to throw, and we threw thousands back into the deeper part of the river, sinking countless floating tins in the process. Ted was very accurate. This was also a favourite spot for lots of my school pals.

At the age of seventeen, I was granted a licence to own a .22 calibre rifle. This was ideal for rabbits, and our bags increased accordingly. Ted was content to retrieve for me and carry the bag. The old game-keeper McKinley would often pay us a shilling for a good rabbit – twopence for Ted, twopence to me and eightpence for Mam, which helped with the family budget.

My mother had, from Ted's early years, written short poems, which she would read to us sometimes. She also invented tales that carried on over several evenings, and to which we would contribute sugges-tions. I remember a favourite epic about three mice – Olywyna mouse, Edwyna mouse and Geraldine mouse. This story engrossed us for many sessions, as it echoed our own adventures. Such wonderful stories helped us all to develop our imaginations and vocabulary. As a result, our interest in literature was awakening – particularly poetry. One of Mam's poems, of which I have the original written on brown paper and dated 1936, reads as follows:

By Edith Hughes
Down by the rippling brook
Where the water flows so softly by,
The trout splash in and out,
And they at once attract the eye,
They are so swift, so sleek, so sly,
I find a shady nook,
And settle down, to read my book.

About this time, Ted would recite poetry that had caught his attention. He also knew the Australian ballad 'Waltzing Matilda' from beginning to end – he once asked me what a jumbuck was – and would sing this from time to time in a strong, tuneful voice, most effectively, little realising that he was singing me out into my future country.

Mother encouraged us to apply ourselves at school, but in my case the call of the hills and moors won out. As one of my school reports read, 'Gerald could be brilliant if he would only concentrate.' Ted and Olwyn could and did, though Ted's real education, until his early teens, was in natural country life. My future lay with aeroplanes and engineering, influenced by my later RAF service. Artistic inspiration simmered, but well below the surface of my practical everyday life. Some of it came out in the odd painting or sketch, but this did not emerge as a sustained interest until later in life, when an ability to paint provided me with a satisfying hobby, for which I am grateful.

Our friendship with the local farmers steadily developed, particularly with Edgar Greenwood, also our milkman, of Burchen Lee Carr Farm, which was situated about halfway up the steep fields above Banksfields. This was an ancient manor house, complete with pack-horse track running through the grounds. We often quietly walked around the old, partially ruined homestead, but we never discharged a gun around occupied farms. I taught Ted the dangers of .22 rifle bullets in particular, which could travel a mile and still do substantial harm. I also taught him never to shoot at anything unless he could be sure the shot would not carry through and damage stock, or anything which might be out of sight. He was quick to learn, and I frequently reminded him of my favourite saying, 'Each day presents a jewel; note it and absorb it, but ignore it at your peril.'

From Burchen Lee Carr we would walk up to Hanging Royd, along to Old Castle and Hey Head, cutting down across the fields to the stream running down from the moors at Foster Clough. One day, halfway down, Ted and I flushed out a rabbit, which ran before we could get a shot at it. To our surprise, the rabbit ran straight for a six-foot dry stone wall, jumped to the top and over it – the only hurdling rabbit I've ever seen.

Just over the field wall, below Hey Head, we established a camping spot on a level area in between the fences, just alongside the stream. We often pitched our Bukta Wanderlust two-man tent on that secluded patch of the clough, and from there hunted below Stoney Lane and along into Han Royd Bank Wood, where we always found rabbits. We would call on Stoney Royd Farm and once saw a stoat in the dry stone wall there. I remember we sat for hours outside a brick outbuilding at the farm where we had previously seen a large rat. Finally, our patience was rewarded when a rat appeared and was promptly shot by Ted – who talked about it to Mam and Dad for days! The farmer gave him a half-dozen eggs for that.

Occasionally my friend Kenward Thomas, son of a local publican, would accompany us with his little dog, Trigger. Ken was a fine shot and loved the hills as much as we did. We had many happy days together. My other pals at this time were Edward Hill and Harry Sutcliffe, who lived at Albert Street – a few doors from Granny Farrar. Harry joined the Army and was killed by enemy action in France early in the war.

Life proceeded at a pleasant pace. The local population was very tolerant and law-abiding. We felt so secure; it never seemed necessary to put a lock and chain on a cycle whenever it was parked in a public place or outside your own home. No one ever gave a second thought to securing their possessions. The people in the village were on modest incomes, working mainly in the several weaving sheds and also in clothing factories such as the one owned by our uncles, Tom and Walter Farrar. Otherwise, they were involved in dairy farming or poultry breeding and similar activities, either locally or in nearby Hebden Bridge or Halifax – few ventured further than that. On the whole, a high standard of public morality was the norm. Even throughout the Depression each helped his neighbour in every possible way. It is quite likely that in such a worrying time of reduced income, with firms on 'short time' and everyone struggling to make ends meet, our society attained a high degree of cooperation and security that has not been known since.

Everyone was very house proud and respectable – good-humoured people with simple tastes. Another world now. All the kids used to go to church – to the Wesleyan or Methodist chapels, which were also generally well attended by adults, mostly women, who knew all the hymns. And at the centre of village life were social activities such as the Easter celebrations, and the concerts and little plays that were put on by the chapels – a chance for everybody to show off their new clothes.

I joined the local Boys' Brigade, which was organised by the Mount Zion Chapel seniors. This entailed weekly attendance for drills and lectures. We were issued with a scout hat and a fine leather belt, but our move away in 1938 saw an end to my involvement. Ted had intended to join the brigade the year we left. He said that he wanted a scout hat like mine, which he thought was like a Mountie's hat – that was the attraction.

During this period Ted went to the Burnley Road Council Primary School, where he was a good student from his early years. He had the capacity to focus on a subject and always made careful notes. He also solidly bombarded me with questions, so in a very positive manner he was responsible for my turning to books – which I did more and more.

As previously mentioned, my school days at Hebden Bridge Central had ended in 1934, when I began work at my uncles' clothing works in Banksfields. The factory was only a five-minute walk from our home, which, incidentally, had been built in 1899, together with many others in Banksfields, originally to house workers for the clothing mill and the adjoining weaving mill, or weaving shed, as we called it.

At weekends we visited relations, or on occasion would take a tram car to the Sowerby Bridge swimming baths – weather permitting. And the family, including Aunty Hilda, would picnic in Redacre Wood and adjacent fields.

Throughout this time, our fishing trips along the canal went steadily on. The two-pound jam jar on our kitchen windowsill was continually restocked with small whiskered gudgeons, caught mainly with our long-handled fishing nets, the net invariably being made from old net curtains. But try as we did to keep the little fish alive for more than a few days, they unfortunately died – to be thrown back into the canal, and the jar restocked. Later on, Ted thought they needed a larger jar and perhaps water from the canal. He would return with half a bucketful, but this extended their little lives by only a day or two. We never found the secret ingredient they required. Later I made Ted a rod with just a hook and line, but no reel. He was ever on the look-out for the large, elusive pike he felt sure lived under the bridge, but we never saw one.

Some years later we were discussing the short lives of the little fish when Ted said, 'You know what the secret element was? It was our removing the little gudgeons from their cool, dark habitat under the canal bridge and exposing them to sunlight in a jam jar.'

My brother was very sociable, with friends in the village. We called frequently on Granny Farrar, who lived nearby, and on Uncle Albert, his wife Minnie and their daughter Glenys, as well as Mam's sister, Hilda. We would also call on Uncle Walter and his family, who lived close, the other side of the recreation ground. So friends and relatives were near and we always found a home from home on our visits.

Later, Ted wrote about playing 'tip cat' with Uncle Albert. A tip cat is a six-inch by one-and-a-half-inch billet of wood balanced on the end of a bat similar to a baseball bat. The billet was flicked into the air; the striker then swings the bat and strikes the billet, or cat. The longest shot wins the competition.

Aunt Hilda gave Ted, when he was five or six, *The Animal Book*, a thick, green, bound volume. Each entry had full information on the animal concerned, plus a good photograph. The book was somewhat beyond Ted's years but he read and absorbed it.

Around this time, my mother often took Ted and Olwyn to Halifax for shopping and sometimes I joined them. Ted's treat was to buy one of the small lead animals sold by Woolworths at that time – admirably modelled and painted. He gradually acquired enough – a lion, tiger, giraffe etc. – to cover the full extent of the flat-topped fender in the sitting room. Mother would always take us to Workman's café afterwards to eat the delicious meat pies for which the Calder Valley was famous.

Mam sometimes took Olwyn and Ted to the seaside during these years – Blackpool, Morecambe and, from 1948, Flamborough Head, where Hilda had a caravan. Ted surely saw his first live wild animals in Blackpool Zoo.

With all this information on the range and beauty of the creatures we share our world with, Ted's fascination with local beasts and birds was widened at a very early age. He used to model animals in plasticine and became very good at it. His lifelong friend Dan Huws recalls that, many years later, Ted made a whole zoo of plasticine animals for Dan's small daughter while visiting the Huws family. The models were so good they kept them on the mantelpiece for a year or two until they disintegrated.

In Devon, in 1966 or 1967, Ted produced two fine clay models of a jaguar, which were fired and glazed by the North Tawton postman, a friend and a potter, who also provided the modelling clay. He gave one to me and the other to Olwyn. A jaguar was, of course, the subject of one of Ted's best-known poems, with those powerful lines: 'He spins from the bars, but there's no cage to him / More than to the visionary his cell...' My jaguar, to quote another line from Ted's poem, seemed to be 'on a short, fierce fuse', whereas Olwyn's was running free. When we visited Ted in Devon many years later, on display in the front room were some models of animals made by his son Nicholas while he was at school at Bedales.

The jaguar, modelled by Ted and fired by a local potter, which Ted gave me.

For a while there was a great interest in kite flying in the village, and the sloping fields rising above Banksfields were perfect with their steady breezes, resulting in some spectacular flights. Ted helped me up in the attic with the construction of several kits – each one slightly larger than the last. We had settled on the popular coffin-lid shape, which seemed to be the most efficient, and with the correct tail to balance it, it flew very well.

Kites often reached a height of two hundred feet or more and were very stable in the high winds. We lost a few when we flew them up on Sugar Loaf Hill, when strong gusts would break the string and float the kite over the nearby moor. I remember a local man flying a six-foot kite, held by a strong cord. It flew enormously high, much higher than any of ours. It was exciting sport, but after a year or so the kite craze waned and some other pastime took over. However, climbing those hills and running around after kites and gliders kept us all very fit. I wonder if the young people of that valley still have the healthy sport now that we enjoyed then?

The annual Co-op sports day was very popular, with prizes awarded for running, sack races and the like. Ted ran and won a large jar of strawberry jam. I remember Mam calling out, 'Run faster, run faster.' The following day he proudly collected the jar of jam. When this was emptied it joined another on our kitchen windowsill – to be stocked with our fishing catch. Simple things, simple pleasures, but all combining to make a happy, healthy lifestyle. Life in Mytholmroyd was full of interest.

Chapter Three

Growing Up

In the years 1927–38, we enjoyed warm summers, and on one memorable occasion my mother took us down to Stubbs Mill Dam to bathe. Olwyn recalls Ted's first swim there: 'I was sitting with Mam and Ted was paddling at the edge of the dam – he couldn't swim then – when suddenly he was in quite deep water. Mam tore down to get him out, but he was swimming away happily, doggy-paddle style – his first ever swim.'

There was a dramatic incident in 1937 when, one warm weekend, Dad joined us for a picnic and swim at the dam. He dived in, but the water was murky and not as deep as he thought, having being stirred up by the bathers. He quickly surfaced, bleeding from injuries to his arms and chest, and it transpired that he'd dived onto a rusty old bicycle that had been thrown into the dam years before. That accident didn't surprise Olwyn, who always felt the dam was dirty and dangerous. After that lesson Mam would generally take Ted and Olwyn to the Sowerby Bridge public baths.

I would often join them, and sometimes Aunt Hilda would too, usually on the way to do a bit of shopping in Halifax. That's where I learnt to swim when I was quite a young child. We also swam a lot in a little pool in the rocky stream up in Crag Vale, where we often went for picnics and where the water was clear and lovely. I remember those swims as a paradise – much better than the dam.

My memories of the years 1932–38 deserve a more detailed recall than I can manage, but despite the onset of the Great Depression, in retrospect those years seem golden. Our mother, always calm, amazingly selfless, marvellously even-tempered – Ted was very like her in temperament – was a constant friend to her children. We thought all mothers were like her, but no one realised what a rare jewel she was. Olwyn recalls that our mother had psychic tendencies and sometimes saw 'ghosts', but several of these events occurred when I was away from home serving in the RAF and I can only remember one such occasion myself – when she claimed to have woken in the night and seen an apparition of her younger sister Miriam at the foot of her bed. She had, in fact, been deeply distraught when Miriam passed away as they were very close. I have to say she didn't seem shocked by the visitation.

Olwyn has other clear memories, which she graphically described in a note she sent me recently:

Besides the ghostly form when Tom, her brother, was dying in an ambulance on the way to hospital, I recall the following. On the night of D-day she was sleepless much of the night sitting at her bedroom window in Mexborough. Around the church opposite our house, the sky was full of little crosses of light, coming and going. Many young men from the area lost their lives that night.

She goes on:

When my parents first moved to The Beacon in Heptonstall, my mother saw a ghostly form on the first few nights. She concluded it must be Mrs Normanton, the former owner of the house, looking for her daughter, who had sold the house to my parents. When the shadowy entity reappeared she clearly announced the new address of the daughter in Hebden Bridge. It didn't appear again.

Olwyn suggests that this might have been an inherited gift. In the First World War, Uncle Walter was missing for quite a while. Then, one morning, Annie, his mother, came down to breakfast happier than for weeks. Walter had appeared at her bedside and told her that he had been injured but was recovering in France in hospital.

Dad was a hard-working joiner in the portable building trade. I remember his 5.30 a.m. early rising, him lighting the fire to warm up the kitchen area for us, coughing when smoking his first cigarette, the clatter of the coal bucket; then, after a quick breakfast – laid out the evening before by Mother – he would be off to catch his bus down on Burnley Road to begin his day's work for F. & H. Sutcliffe in Hebden Bridge.

Dad was so fortunate to have managed to survive the Great War, which had seen the decimation of his school friends and the youth of the area. I remember him as a greatly caring father, but generally reticent when it came to talking about his near-death experiences of that war. From time to time, though, he would casually mention details about his service in a low-key way, such as how he used to go into no-man's land at night and bring in the wounded. Once, he brought a high-ranking officer in who told Dad he would recommend him for the VC, but nothing came of it. Ted and I always regretted the fact that we never pressed him more to talk even more about his experiences, though what he told us was horrific enough. I remember that Dad had always felt the Australians were particularly fine soldiers. He often said that.

The First World War was a continual source of fascination for us, and the story of the six young men from Hebden Bridge who perished in it became the subject of one of Ted's most powerful and moving poems.

Six Young Men

The celluloid of a photograph holds them well –
Six young men, familiar to their friends.
Four decades that have faded and ochre-tinged
This photograph have not wrinkled the faces or the hands.
Though their cocked hats are not now fashionable,
Their shoes shine. One imparts an intimate smile,
One chews a grass, one lowers his eyes, bashful,
One is ridiculous with cocky pride –
Six months after this picture they were all dead.

All are trimmed for a Sunday jaunt. I know

That bilberried bank, that thick tree, that black wall,
Which are there yet and not changed. From where these sit
You hear the water of seven streams fall
To the roarer in the bottom, and through all
The leafy valley a rumouring of air go.
Pictured here, their expressions listen yet,
And still that valley has not changed its sound
Though their faces are four decades under the ground.

This one was shot in an attack and lay
Calling in the wire, then this one, his best friend,
Went out to bring him in and was shot too;
And this one, the very moment he was warned
From potting at tin-cans in no-man's land,
Fell back dead with his rifle-sights shot away.
The rest, nobody knows what they came to,
But come to the worst they must have done, and held it
Closer than their hope; all were killed.

Here see a man's photograph,
The locket of a smile, turned overnight
Into the hospital of his mangled last
Agony and hours; see bundled in it
His mightier-than-a-man dead bulk and weight:
And on this one place which keeps him alive
(In his Sunday best) see fall war's worst
Thinkable flash and rending, onto his smile
Forty years rotting into soil.

That man's not more alive whom you confront
And shake by the hand, see hale, hear speak loud,
Than any of these six celluloid smiles are,
Nor prehistoric or fabulous beast more dead;
No thought so vivid as their smoking-blood:
To regard this photograph might well dement, Such
contradictory permanent horrors here
Smile from the single exposure and shoulder out
One's own body from its instant and heat.

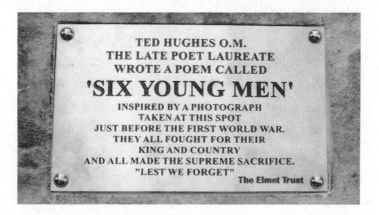

It was around this time that Ted and I developed a passion for model boats. The lead obtained from our bullet melting had solved most of our problems with the fitting of a strip to the keel, as previously mentioned, but our boat building changed after Dad gave us a model steam engine one Christmas.

Apart from turning its large red flywheel, it didn't do anything special, so we decided to try to use the engine to power a boat.

The problem of a suitable hull was a difficult one. However, Dad suggested that he could supply a suitably hollowed out piece of pine wood, and asked me to do a sketch. I measured up the steam engine and how much space I would require for the relocated piston and flywheel, eventually producing a rough drawing showing the engine happily chugging away in a deep hull.

All this was finally solved when, by a bit of bargaining, I obtained the hull of what had been a replica galleon, which had lost its masts and deck. However, the remaining hull – about two feet long – was in good shape and ideal for our purpose. We detached the steam engine from its base plate, installed it in the hull and arranged the piston and flywheel to engage with a propeller shaft. It wasn't easy, and I remember the problems we faced. Firstly the shaft was too light, causing it to twist when the engine was fired up. This was solved with a heavier shaft with a crank end that engaged with the spokes on the engine flywheel, to which we attached a small propeller – cut from a cocoa tin lid. The shaft was installed by bending the end to secure the flimsy tin propeller. We tried the new boat in the canal, finding first that it leaked water through the shaft hole – we packed it with Vaseline, which fixed it. Then the propeller gave trouble. A simple blob of solder would have solved it, but we had no access to solder, or equipment, so we struggled on until finally we adapted a part from our Meccano set – good old Meccano, you can make anything with it! We named the boat *Tugboat Annie.*

It was a great success and once started would chug along at a slow walking pace. It was controlled by setting the rudder to guide the boat away from us, but was kept straight by attaching a length of string to the prow. Ted would march along keeping the string taut and the boat on course. It was good fun and quite an engineering lesson for us. To make it return, we simply turned the rudder and proceeded in a similar fashion.

I clearly remember that when Ted was about seven years old, we were sailing the little boat on the canal, when a man walking by said, 'I would like to buy that boat from you. What do you want for it?' Quick as a flash Ted said, 'Sorry, it's not for sale,' and of course it wasn't. Life's wondrous moments cannot be bartered. We sailed this boat right up to the time of our leaving Mytholmroyd. I remember seeing it on a shelf in our garage in Mexborough – one of my clear memories of home before I left for north Africa, when I was twenty-two. But I don't know what happened to *Tugboat Annie.* That's how dreams are, I suppose. They just are, and then they're gone.

Our hunting trips in 1937–38 became longer – lasting all day, in fact. We also went camping over the weekends, covering the moors and hills from the Skip Inn to Midgley, the farms along the moor's edge being particularly good for rabbits. While on the Heights Road moor's edge, we saw plenty of hawks – kestrels mainly, but also sparrowhawks and the occasional peregrine falcon.

Ted and I began to sketch birds and animals. He developed an interesting style, much more detailed than mine right from the beginning, and took great care to get the proportions right. In 1936 I had purchased a Box Brownie camera from a friend with the intention of photographing wildlife, but as film was expensive and developing it even more so, I took very few snaps. Sadly, most of these have been lost or given away. I remember only three. One is of Ted standing at the corner of our house, another of Olwyn holding at arm's length a stoat I had shot that day, with the third being the group of Mother, Ted and Olwyn at the Stubbs Mill Dam, taken at one of our picnics.

Our mother was always keen to try and develop our artistic abilities, and at an early age arranged for me to have piano lessons. I was not enthusiastic and they didn't last long. Later, Olwyn too had lessons. She was not particularly gifted either, but after the lessons were ended, she knew a few simple pieces. I remember Beethoven's 'Für Elise' and one or two pieces of Chopin. She occasionally used to play her small repertoire through the years.

Ted never had piano lessons. I think Mam must have concluded that her family were not pianists, but this was possibly a mistake. One day in Mexborough Olwyn was playing one of her pieces when Ted came into the room and told her he was composing a symphony and would she like to hear the opening. He sat at the piano and, with one hand but no hesitations, played for a few minutes a charming and impressive melody. Olwyn was totally astonished. 'I always think of W. H. Auden's lines in connection with this incident,' she told me:

> The youngest son, the youngest son,
> was certainly no wise one
> but could surprise one.

Ted was, in fact, a very wise child, but he certainly could surprise one. By his mid-teens he had become devoted to Beethoven and purchased the nine symphonies one by one, then the late quartets. All his life he revered Beethoven as, for him, the finest of composers.

But I must return to the heady days of 1937, when Ted and I had three days camping at Crimsworth Dean, where we enjoyed exploring the unfamiliar area. We pitched our tent in a sheltered dell, which I thought to be a disused quarry, with a rock face behind the site giving protection from the wind.

This spot had been recommended to us by our Uncle Walter, who regularly camped there before the First World War with his brother Tom and two friends. It was a quiet, wooded area with farm fields beginning about fifty yards beyond a dry stone wall, where, on the second day, we found a dead fox under a deadfall trap. These were traps with a heavy rock or concrete slab set at the top that crashed on the animal's head when it took the bait.

There was an abundance of birdlife, with barn owls calling at night. The local farmer, a friend of Uncle Walt's, gave us permission to shoot on his land, but despite our best efforts we left without firing a shot. Although we saw a few rabbits in the long field grass, they eluded us.

It was a strange, eerie place with wild beautiful scenery. After the drama of the fox in the trap, Ted had a restless night and insisted on telling me of a vivid dream about an old lady and a fox cub that, the old lady said, had been orphaned by the trap. I've always felt that this incident marked the beginning of Ted's great interest in the fox, and his hatred of deadfall traps. He later explored his dream in a story called 'The Deadfall', included in his collected short stories, *Difficulties of a Bridegroom*.

In those days we led very busy lives. When not at school, there was always fishing in the canal, or playing football or using the swings and slides at the nearby recreation ground – the Rec, as we called it. In the evenings, small groups of my local pals would gather under the gas street light and talk a while. A very innocent lifestyle, thinking back, when whip and top were the rage and children would play with 'hoop and sher', a steel ring about three feet in diameter, controlled by a short length of steel rod with a twist at the end to maintain control of the hoop as we ran along.

Sugar Loaf Hill, where Ted and I flew our kites.

One day Ted and I walked around the top rim of Scout Rock. It was a mild, white-clouded and blue-sky day and we took my rifle. We first carefully explored the area at the base of the rock, but saw no rabbits. We then found our way up and out onto the fields above the rock, and once up there we sat a while with the Mytholmroyd township spread out below us, absorbing the view of our house and Banksfields rising on the other side of the valley.

The Mount Zion Chapel looked small from up there, almost hiding our home. Walking further on, we met a farmer who told us how his son had shot a wood pigeon flying over there and that, after taking the shot, the pigeon had set its wing to glide away down the rock to crash far below, and what a walk it was to recover it!

We seldom crossed the valley. The Scout Rock area was wooded and a likely location for rabbits, but as it was not on our side of the valley we visited it less often than the hills adjacent to our home. Nevertheless, the high brooding ridge of the rock was there, every day, and invoked our curiosity. We imagined that in the past centuries there must have been a great deal of drama in our little valley, and that the rock would have seen its fair share of it – certainly in the Middle Ages with the ceaseless unrest following the Norman occupation of Britain, and earlier during the Roman conquests.

Not far away on the moor, on the rock's side of the Mytholmroyd valley, a Roman military road passed by on its way north. A portion of this road had been excavated and cleaned up. It was visited by organised parties of children from all the schools in the area. What a powerful history lesson we had on the day our class made the short bus trip. It was not surprising that, years later, boys rabbiting at the rock found a hoard of Roman coins. This was widely reported by local newspapers and no doubt led to further searching using metal detectors. But by that time we had long since left the valley, so we missed the exciting find – right on our old doorstep.

When I recall my impressions of the rock, I remember Ted scampering up from his room saying, 'I'll see what the weather's like.' Then he'd climb onto my small table, which was almost directly beneath the skylight, and, carefully avoiding my bits and pieces on the table, would open the skylight two or three notches and give me a weather report, such as, 'The sky is clear above Scout Rocks, so we should be OK.'

Around Christmas time, heavy snowfalls were common, and all the local children owned sledges. A favourite place was the long, sloping Co-op field. Sledging at speed down here was great sport. We went higher – speeding over the bump – but that bottom field was the favourite spot for all the local children. Ted loved it there on those frosty, crisp evenings. We had a rough sledge to begin with, but Dad built a more comfortable one, with broader steel runners, a cross-bar for our feet and good rope reins. Ted sat in front of me and we would stay out sledging until late in the evening, returning home cold and sometimes wet, leaving our sledge in the short archway near our back door.

One evening there was a sudden snowfall on the slope – probably a snap frost – and Ted and I found ourselves rocketing down the sloping field at a far greater speed than usual. Coming to the end of the run, I vainly tried to slow the speeding sledge by digging my feet into the snow, but on this occasion it was as hard as ice and I was unable to stop. We finished up crashing through the wire-and-paling fence surrounding the hen pen at the bottom of the field, but were fortunately uninjured. We spent half an hour fixing that fence! What saved us was the long, projecting front of the sledge with its sturdy cross-bar for the feet. After that incident I thought seriously about some method of braking for the sledge, but never got around to implementing any modification.

Ted and I often talked about those days, and in an interview included in the BBC television programme 'Close Up', shown at Christmas 1998, shortly after his death, Ted spoke about the strong impression they left on his young mind.

———•◆•———

My employment with the uncles proceeded steadily, with my promotion from window cleaner (there were about two hundred small windows to clean!) and floor sweeper, to working in the cutting room. There I was permitted to cut specified lengths of cloth and stack them prior to patterns being outlined in chalk on the top sheet and the resultant shapes then cut out on a band saw, which was operated mainly by Fred Wilcox and Jack Crossley, trusted long-time employees.

My mother did some work for my uncles too, and an arrangement was made with her whereby she would help out with large orders of sportswear by working at home in her little sewing room, above the front door of 1 Aspinall Street. Many were the times when I shouldered large bundles of flannel sports trousers and carried them down the steep back-door factory steps and out into Banksfields to deliver one lot to Mother. The work carried out by her was mainly the time-consuming sewing on of hooks and eyes by hand, with occasional machining work finished on her pedal-operated Singer sewing machine. Once home, I would climb our stairs to her small room, sit and chat a while, then return to the factory with her finished work. This contribution certainly helped with our sparse budget, but that was how people worked in the Depression. Just to keep financially afloat, everyone chipped in as best they could – nothing was wasted. There was no gambling; every penny was treasured, and somehow we made it through that desperate period, which cannot be imagined by anyone who has not experienced it.

After our move to Mytholmroyd, we still paid visits to our Granny (Polly) Hughes in her little sweet shop at 4 King Street, Mytholm, usually going there by bus. Christmas time was always exciting. Granny never failed to provide gifts for all the family – a doll and chocolates for Olwyn; a box of lead animals, or soldiers, for Ted; chocolates for Mother; and for me there were Liquorice Allsorts or toffees. Dad always received cigarettes.

We would return to Mytholmroyd a few days before Christmas laden with parcels, which were carefully hidden away from Ted and Olwyn until Mam and I, on Christmas Eve, would creep into their bedrooms and fill their pillowcases with presents. What happy cries were heard early on Christmas morning. Ted would come tearing up the stairway to my attic, jump on my bed and gleefully show me his presents and Olwyn would follow – both wanting to share any edible goodies they had. This would take care of the early morning, after which we would all help Mam with the setting up of the table for Christmas dinner. These are memories of a wonderfully happy time. Later on we would visit Uncle Albert, his wife Minnie and their daughter, Glenys, who lived at 19 Aspinall Street, and then move on to see Auntie Hilda, who lived with Granny Farrar in Albert Street.

There were few cars in Mytholmroyd. I would cycle up the Highway to school in Hebden Bridge and see no more than half a dozen cars, along with the occasional bus or delivery van. So cycling was a pleasure, with little of the traffic we have now. Of course, there were horses and carts travelling the roads in the valley – the horse still maintaining a tenuous hold on its much-loved, well-proven place in our lives and economy.

In 1936 I joined the Hebden Bridge Cycling Club, and every other weekend I went with a group of a dozen or more pals for cycling trips out to Grassington, Kettlewell and other spots of scenic interest. I now possessed a Sun Wasp bicycle, purchased from William Dugdale's shop in Hebden Bridge for three pounds. It was paid for by Granny Hughes as a Christmas present. Ted took over this fine cycle in 1940 when I joined the RAF.

In mid-1937 there was a slump in trade, with most factories working only two or three days a week. My father also went on short time, as it was called. He came home one day and said that he had applied for work with the government on a building contract in Glamorgan in south Wales. A work friend had also applied. They were successful, and in a short time Dad was on his way. I remember carrying his heavy oblong tool box down the hill to the bus stop and saying my goodbyes to him. Mother, left to cope with three young children, missed him badly and, to use her own words, 'was miserable'.

My uncles' clothing factory also went on short time to about three days a week in 1937. This meant I found myself with lots of spare time, and my forays after rabbits increased correspondingly. I was conscious of the need to conserve all our resources now that my pay had been reduced to twenty-five shillings a week. How we managed to exist on such a low income I do not know – my pittance, together with my father's, amounting to four pounds or so weekly – but somehow Mam always managed to care for us with warm, loving kindness and good humour, and to produce wholesome meals. Our milkman, I remember, was generous – leaving more milk than we requested. Most of our food supplies were purchased from the Co-op shop, which was just over the canal bridge a hundred yards from our home. I remember we ate lots of porridge, Shredded Wheat, fruit, vegetables and fish – as well as the rabbits I managed to shoot. I did most of the shopping, with Ted's help.

Chapter Four

Mexborough

After our idyllic early years in the lovely Calder
Valley of Hebden Bridge and Mytholmroyd, it
came as a real shock to Ted, Olwyn and me when,
in 1938, our parents announced that we would be
moving to Mexborough, a mining town then in the
West Riding of Yorkshire. Dad had become homesick
being so far away from us, and when he inherited
some money from his mother, Granny Hughes, he'd
begun looking round for a rundown newsagents with
prospects. Eventually, he'd found one, with a spacious
house attached. It was situated in the town's main
street, on a corner block, with large window space
and a garage, but no garden. It was, Mam wrote, 'a
dark, dirty place when we arrived, all of us travelling
down in the removal van. I remember Dad standing
behind the counter when we walked in, trying to look
confident. We were soon organised.'

My last memory of our old home was of Ted and
me climbing into the open back of the removal van,

Ted holding the cat and sitting facing back over the raised tailboard as we slowly pulled away. A few neighbours and friends were gathered to bid us a sad farewell as the van turned along the front of the stately Mount Zion Chapel, into Midgley Road, and over the Rochdale Canal bridge. We watched our home pass from view. One last glimpse of the canal – where we had launched so many model ships and Ted had become a dedicated fisherman – past the Co-op shop, then on down the hill to the main Burnley Road where, as we turned left, I caught sight of the shoe repair shop to which Ted and I had often taken our clogs and shoes for mending.

Then on the right we passed the home of my schoolfriend George Sainsbury, whose house was also a sweet shop. A hundred yards further was the Royal Oak Hotel, home of Kenward Thomas, another good friend; on up the hill over the canal bridge where another school pal, Billy Royd, lived with his parents, who owned a plumbing business there. Over our canal again, the public recreation ground on the left, with its fondly remembered swings and slide, and the football ground where I had shown unfulfilled promise for a career in soccer. Then along to where my shooting friend Cedric Lomas and his brother worked in their family business. Next, past dear Uncle Walter's imposing 'Southfield' house at Ewood Gate – the extreme point of my old paper delivery round

– and proceeding on through Halifax to our destination, Mexborough.

We were so well aware that we were leaving all our relatives and close friends behind and Ted and I watched the familiar hills above Banksfields slide from view with much emotion – it was, after all, the landscape of our childhood. I remember saying, 'Never mind, Ted, we'll be back, it's not very far to Mexborough' – little realising that we would never again take up that carefree lifestyle we were leaving behind. Everything would change. Olwyn tells me she cried for two weeks when we arrived there, though we both remember Ted taking it more calmly.

In Mexborough, everything was on a far larger scale than we were used to in Mytholmroyd, where there were several churches and chapels, but very few pubs. I only remember the ancient Dusty Miller and don't recall any betting shops. In Mexborough proportions were reversed. Mexborough was a mining town, and the miners and railway workers were great spenders. The racing journal, known as 'The Pink'Un' (it was printed on pink paper), was a big seller, and the townsfolk perused it avidly before placing bets at the betting shops. They also spent a lot of their earnings in the town's many pubs. Their homes – the little I saw of them – appeared crowded and lacked the house-proud style of Mytholmroyd, which now seemed on another planet. This, perhaps, was a result of their spending. The other side of town, however, was pretty middle-class and sedate. There were several cinemas, well attended, and repertory companies would arrive with plays, which our mother took us to from time to time. On top of this, the grammar school organised trips to Sheffield for concerts and more established theatrical companies. There was a large and very good public library.

Missing from Mexborough were the Mytholmroyd events that marked the slow turning of the year – the outdoor Easter performances of the paysagers in Midgley with their archaic drama, the spring gathering of docks (for dock pudding, eaten at breakfast, a local cure for all winter's ills and possibly unique to that valley). At that time, the children would scour the area for docks and go from door to door selling crammed carrier bags of them for sixpence. On May Day there was maypole dancing, followed by the summer gathering of bilberries on the moors. There were the council processions too – children and adults dressed up to represent a particular theme and driven on carts around the main streets – and the accompanying field day, where races were arranged for the children and stalls sold various tempting snacks and knick-knacks. We also missed the special services and chapel concerts with the children's chorus, and the entire area's preparations for the big Guy Fawkes fire on the open area in front of our house, where we set off fireworks and roasted potatoes round the edges. All those enjoyable, involving kinds of activities disappeared with the Mexborough move.

For all that, my parents seemed pleased with the change and my father, always an early riser, soon had the various paper delivery rounds organised. Before long we adapted happily enough to our new surroundings and friends. It was wonderful having a paper shop with all the comics and girls' and boys' magazines on hand. We weathered the change well. Ted always made friends easily and local boys living near the shops – some shopkeepers' children like us – used to come and play in the side road near the house.

Soon after we moved, Ted started going to a Saturday morning film show – exclusively cowboy films – at a nearby cinema locally known as the 'Flea Pit'. He went with friends from the local infant school, and indeed the audience was mostly young boys. The films he saw there were probably the inspiration for an early poem, printed later in the grammar school magazine, about an Indian–cowboy exchange that ends:

> Knee-deep in blood where he had to paddle
> Stood Diamond Ace with an empty saddle.

First Olwyn and then Ted won scholarships to the excellent local grammar school in Mexborough at exactly the right time in their lives. John Fisher, a fine English teacher there, spotted Ted's talent even at that early age and was excited by it. When I met him in later life he told me he always felt that Ted would be very special. A photo of Ted, taken at school in 1940, clearly shows his calm, serious expression, which changed very little throughout his life. He's sporting his favourite pullover, which he wore on many of our fishing and rabbit-shooting days together. Ted quickly became a keen reader – particularly of myth and folk-lore, and, early on, of Kipling's verse.

Ted vividly recalled these early influences in a letter, written in 1978, to the critic Keith Sagar:

First to take an interest in my writing was our form mistress in my first class – a Miss Mcleod, who was also the Headmistress. Fine looking woman – I fell in love with her, somewhat. Next was Pauline Mayne – then about 23. She touched off my passion to write poetry. I used to write long lolloping Kiplingesque sagas, about all kinds of things. She pointed to a phrase – describing the hammer of a wildfowlers' gun breaking in the cold 'with frost-chilled snap'. 'That's poetry,' she said. And I thought, well if that's poetry that's the way I think so I can give you no end of it. She became a close friend of my family's – still is I suppose. Then came John Fisher – demobbed. For a while it was Pauline and John together. I was in love with both, so they could teach me anything. John F. had only to exclaim about the unearthly mightiness of Beethoven – whom I had never knowingly listened to – for me to become such a sotted addict of Beethoven that his music dominated my life till I left University & lost my gramophone & radio. Even so, ever since, it has preoccupied me at some level. I still listen to it in preference to anything else. That's education, I suppose.

Of course, another strong influence on Ted at this stage was Olwyn, as he later acknowledged: 'With my brother gone, I came under the influence of my sister. She was ahead of me at school and an academic star. She also had a forceful personality. Also, as it happened, she had a sophisticated taste in poetry.'

Ted never really enjoyed organised sports, but like me he became a keen cyclist and he joined the Denaby Wheelers, through a friend at the grammar school. The cycling club went on long rides in the area, their bikes adapted for speed with drop handlebars and so on. Ted was quite enthusiastic about this for a time in his early teens. He also cycled seriously later, when at Cambridge.

For my part, after four years in the wholesale clothing manufacturing business, and those three long years of evening classes, I found myself in an area where there was little, or indeed none, of the same employment available. However, one of Dad's customers, who was a qualified foreman fitter and turner working for Bessemer Steel Works in nearby Rotherham, suggested I work with him as a trainee fitter. After an interview at Bessemer, I was employed there. What a steep learning curve that was – from making overalls for workers to wearing them in an engineering environment. I had only been three months with Bessemer Steel when an incident occurred that again changed the direction of my life.

One day, in a corner of the enormous factory area, I was cleaning grease from my hands when the cleaning rag was caught in a moving belt driven by an electric motor. In a split second, my right hand was pulled onto the belt and held fast against the motor drive pulley. Fortunately, the belt was well worn, so instead of taking my hand and arm in, it began to slip. I was alone, with only a crane operator high up within sight. I turned – one hand held by the pulley – to see if I could reach the switchboard on which there were many switches. I could only reach one, and with just my fingernail, I closed the switch. By blessed luck, it just happened to be the right one. Still held firm, I waved to the overhead crane operator who quickly climbed down his ladder and, with his help, I carefully extracted my bleeding hand from between the belt and pulley wheel. After visiting the factory first aid room, I was driven by the engineer to Mexborough Hospital, and my parents were notified.

My hand was operated on for a broken little finger and deep lacerations. I was fortunate to get out of that one lightly. Mam came in after the operation and her first remark was, 'I knew you were tall, Gerald, but you looked ten feet long on that table.' I recovered after about six weeks and a couple more hospital treatments.

During my recuperation, a family friend, Victor, invited me to help him run a garage situated in Barnet, just north of London. When my injury was healed, I took the train for Barnet, where it had been arranged for me to stay next to the garage in the spare bedroom of an elderly lady – a dear, caring person with whom I got along extremely well. She was a widow, and kept a crow in a large cage in her sitting room. She said it was good company and talked to it, and it to her.

At the garage, Victor, a qualified motor mechanic, allowed me to assist in the various repair works needed, and I quickly learnt about cars and their engines. I purchased a motorcycle for five pounds – a Levis – and on this I explored the local area. I was fortunate in that at the time a team of professional motorcycle riders were testing a new make of motorcycle, driving non-stop for two weeks, night and day, between Barnet and Manchester. One of these drivers – resting between journeys – examined my bike and said that he would be pleased to teach me the finer points of riding. He turned out to be Ken Bills, winner of the Isle of Man TT race the year before. He gave me several valuable lessons on the race track in a large nearby field, which was quite a thrill.

I wrote to Ted and explained what I was doing, but he was not happy that I had the motorbike and pleaded with me to sell it, saying that if I wanted to explore the country lanes I should cycle, but not ride a motorbike under any circumstances. He said he hadn't slept properly since I told him about the lessons from Ken Bills.

For all this, I was still yearning for a return to a life in the countryside, and I answered an advertisement posted by a head keeper in Devon in *The Gamekeeper* magazine for a second keeper for the coming season. I was offered the position and happily accepted. Though Vic at the garage had taught me well, a training which helped me in many ways in the coming years, again it was goodbye time, and I took the train to Exeter in Devon.

Upon arrival in Exeter, I found that the bus to Alphington, my destination, left an hour later. As it was a sunny day I decided to walk, and off I went, carrying my little green suitcase. After being directed by a farm worker, I arrived at the end of a tree-lined lane to be met by the keeper's thirteen-year-old daughter, Coral, who, knowing my train arrival time, had waited for me. She competently tied my small case onto the carrier of her cycle and we walked back along the lovely Devon lane to their cottage, set on the edge of a densely wooded hill with a garden and dog kennel on the lower side of the lane, where Coral introduced me to her parents.

The head keeper, Mr Percy Jackson, and his wife welcomed me with a cup of tea, and after a talk about the job, showed me my upstairs bedroom. I settled in after that first meeting as if in my own home, and the warm, friendly atmosphere never changed during my entire ten-month stay with them.

In the meantime, busy days were ahead for Percy and me. He explained my responsibilities and walked me around the boundaries of the Peamore Estate, introducing me to the farmers on the extensive properties who were involved in the shooting season. Our immediate work was organising the many pheasant coops on the rearing field, situated on the edge of a thickly wooded area. We had a small shed for the storage of feed for the parent hens and hungry chicks. I was given a double twelve-gauge shotgun to deter predators – which I seldom used except on feral cats (twice) and a stoat that cunningly made its way among the pheasant chicks by taking advantage of a heavy shower of rain to disguise a quick raid. The same tactic was used once by a sparrowhawk that came in during heavy rainfall, made a kill and was off with it. Although I missed that one, I was impressed by the hawk's well-planned attack.

We reared about a thousand Chinese ring-necked pheasants, and had a 90 per cent success rate. When the young birds were mature enough, they were relocated with a dozen hens for company to various areas of the large estate and neighbouring farms in order to form a nucleus of birds for the coming shooting season. This was, of course, the whole idea of the rearing exercise. The transition from rearing field to a hopeful dispersal on the wider reaches of the estate is one of the ongoing problems for gamekeepers wherever they are. An indiscreet placement of birds can result in the loss of most of that relocated stock, as they will quickly assess where their best interests lie.

One such instance comes to mind which occurred when we relocated birds to what had been, in the past, a proven suitable covert. We found later that a nearby farm, outside the boundaries of our estate, had planted an enormous field of peas and beans. The ripe crop coincided with the shooting period, and unfortunately the birds had shown a liking for this new source of food, leaving us with extremely poor bag results from that area. Overall, though, the shooting syndicate enjoyed a good season in 1939, the last before the war. The day of the final shoot, the bag was laid out in the courtyard with celebratory

1 Aspinall Street, Mytholmroyd, West Yorkshire, where Ted was born.

ABOVE LEFT Ted with Olwyn and Mam, Mytholmroyd, circa 1936.
ABOVE RIGHT In my gamekeeping days on the Peamore estate, Devon, 1938.

ABOVE LEFT Home on leave from the Nottingham City Police, just before leaving for Australia, 1947.
ABOVE RIGHT Ted with his pal John Wholey, Conisbrough, West Yorkshire, 1948.

Mam and Dad with Ted while on leave from National Service in the RAF, circa 1949.

Ted and Mam, taken on the same occasion.

Olwyn, Ted and me, circa 1946.

All ready to go on our Wales trip. Ted is in the back seat; Joan with me in the front. Brixton, London, 1952.

On that same trip: Ted giving Joan an early morning wake-up call after a night in our Bukta Wanderlust tent – the same one Ted and I used in Banksfields in the 1930s.

What a catch! Ted in his Errol Flynn pose, south Devon, 1952.

A nostalgic return with Ted in 1952 to the pond on the Crookhill Estate near Mexborough – the inspiration for his poem 'Pike'.

ABOVE LEFT Ted while at Cambridge University, 1953.
ABOVE RIGHT Olwyn when a student at London University, 1954.

ABOVE LEFT Ted on degree day, 1954.
ABOVE RIGHT Ted and Sylvia with Mam and Dad at The Beacon, Heptonstall, autumn 1956.

ABOVE LEFT Ted and Sylvia at The Beacon, Heptonstall, autumn 1956.
ABOVE RIGHT Ted skinning a badger, with Nick behind him, Court Green, 1966.

ABOVE LEFT Ted presenting the pelt – Frieda beside him and our dad in the background, 1966.
ABOVE RIGHT Me with Assia Wevill in Devon, October 1966, photo by Ted.

The brothers
Hughes at
London Zoo,
autumn 1970.

Ted, Frieda and
Nick at Loch
Ness, spring
1971. A family
camping trip
– looking for
the monster!

drinks – a pleasant finale to a successful season, with no accidents.

In September 1939 we listened together to that chilling radio broadcast by the Prime Minister, Neville Chamberlain, and heard that England was at war with Germany – a day which changed all our lives. September was turning out to be a month of lifestyle changes for me and saying my goodbyes to the Jackson family was not easy, as they had been so kind and helpful. I took my leave, promising a return visit after the war – which I made in 1947.

Arriving back home I had a happy reunion with my family. Olwyn and Ted were now well settled in at school, and very involved in sports and plays. For a few weeks, I assisted my parents in their busy shop. My father efficiently handled the newsagent/tobacconist side and had taken on a concession to sell travel, mostly day trips within England. My mother, meanwhile, had emerged as an enterprising and imaginative businesswoman. With regular visits to suppliers in Doncaster, she filled empty counters, shelves and windows with games, toys, stationery goods, dress patterns etc.

My time at home was to be short lived, and on 25 July 1940 I took a train into nearby Sheffield with the intention of joining up in one of the services. On the journey into Sheffield I shared a carriage with a Coldstream Guardsman in uniform with full kit and rifle, on his way to join his regiment. During our conversation he encouraged me to join the guards – but that wasn't to be. When I arrived at the recruiting centre, I found that Army recruiting was suspended for the afternoon. However, the RAF was there, operating at full bore, and I was interviewed and accepted. After passing my medical examination, I was advised that, because of my fitter's training at Bessemer Steel and my weeks in the garage at Barnet, I would be trained as a flight mechanic, and to return home to await instructions.

Two weeks later I was posted to a training unit in Morecambe. I duly arrived and, after being kitted out with uniform etc., commenced basic training, followed by an intense engineering course involving work on aircraft maintenance and repair. Most of that training took place on the nearby airfield, where classes of a dozen or so were instructed in separate groups – about six groups in our hangar. Throughout the course, airfield guard duties were allocated.

In our hangar, two Fairey Battle aircraft were set up, on which we practised structural repairs. As our instructors were specialists in their subjects, our training was extremely detailed and thorough, particularly with regard to hydraulic systems and metal repairs. I had an aptitude for this type of work and, after successfully completing the course, I was posted to Bristol, from where, after several more weeks of

intensive training, I emerged as Aircraftsman 1st Class
Fitter IIA (AC1).

Early in 1941, after the fitter's course, we were given
a long weekend's leave, which I spent with my family in
Mexborough. Ted and I even managed a day's fishing.

With the stress of the war not yet intruding on
our lives, this was the calm before the storm. We all
missed the extended family, who were still living far
from us in the Mytholmroyd area. I felt sad for my
mother, she being such a warm, family-orientated
person. She was plainly missing her younger sister
Hilda and her three brothers and their families. Food
was now strictly rationed, with many items no longer
available in the stores – the armed forces getting first
consideration.

Enemy aircraft activity was slight, with only spas-
modic bombing. One bomb fell on the railway station
while I was there. But a year later Mother described
heavy raids on nearby targets such as Rotherham
when the house shook and her little ornaments
on the shelf over the fireplace were vibrated to the
floor. There were, however, no bombs dropped in
Main Street.

The blackout curfew was carefully adhered to. I
remember on that leave an air raid warden helping
Dad to tape up all the house windows with crosses of
heavy brown tape to minimise flying shards of glass in
case they broke under bombardment. The many shop

windows had all been taped up earlier in the year. Everyone was working full time, and all were apprehensive about the recent German advances in France and elsewhere. But Mexborough was a mining town, with everyone as busy as beavers. The miners were impressive. They worked hard and played hard. If you walked through Mexborough in the evenings you could hear singing coming from the hotel bar rooms, crowded with miners just off their working shift, as black as the coal they worked with, singing their hearts out. I felt proud of their strength of purpose and knew they would hold firm to the very end, if it came to that. This gave me a feeling of comfort for the family I was leaving behind.

My parents had made many friends in their relatively short time in Mexborough, particularly among their customers, as both were friendly, agreeable souls and always relaxed with people. For their part, Ted and Olwyn seemed to be happy at school, and they too had many friends. So I felt confident that they would all weather the coming uncertain times.

Part II

The War Years

Replacing a Rolls-Royce Merlin engine on a Halifax Bomber in the Western Desert, 1943.

Chapter Five

Squadron Life

My new posting came through to report to RAF Station Pershore, in Worcestershire, and unfortunately I missed my train – the only one that day. There was, however, an early morning connection the following day, so off I went to arrive at my destination one day late, which resulted in my being immediately placed on a charge by the RAF Police.

Standing in front of my new commanding officer, I might have fared better had I not said, when the officer asked my reason for being a day late reporting for duty, 'Well, sir, I missed my train, so I decided to catch the next morning's connection.' That did it. He grimaced and then exploded, 'Oh, you did, did you, you decided. Well, AC1 Hughes, I am the one who makes the decisions in this squadron, and I've decided to give you seven days full pack, reporting to the guard room early morning, noon and evening, besides which you will perform your duties as required, starting tomorrow at 6.00 a.m. Dismiss.'

And so my squadron life began. I did not get into trouble again during my six years' service. About a month later, I met the officer again, who acknowledged my best salute and said, 'I see you are settling in, ACı Hughes, carry on.'

One day I was in nearby Worcester with a young lady whom I had previously met at a dance, and we took a stroll in the lovely public park. Sitting and chatting, oblivious to everything else, we were enjoying our privacy when, after about twenty minutes, all the bushes around us suddenly moved – each bush revealing a fully armed soldier. They cheerfully waved and one said, 'OK, carry on,' before they marched off – a bizarre, never-to-be-forgotten incident.

Pershore was an Operational Training Unit, and I got on well there, enjoying working on the fine Vickers Wellington aircraft. I was at Pershore for about seven months, and during this time a few of us were sent to the Vickers factory at Weybridge for a further course of instructions on the airframe of the Wellington – its control systems, hydraulics etc. While there, my pal Jock and I made a quick half-day visit to London where, unfortunately, we were caught up in an air raid and had to seek cover in a London Underground station. Here we found the platforms crowded with Londoners who appeared to be there on a semi-permanent basis – some had bedding and blankets and baskets of food. There were many children. So we had first-hand close contact with a different aspect of the war. That memory would come back vividly to me during the years I spent in north Africa. I never forgot that those Londoners endured constant air raids with resultant heavy casualties.

Back in Pershore, work resumed after the Vickers visit, and one unusual incident occurred while I was working on a Wellington one day. The refuelling team arrived and, after filling up one side, the petrol bowser was being driven around the tail of the plane when, as it passed the tail section, I felt a small but noticeable shudder move through the aircraft. I observed from the cockpit that the bowser was in position on the wing, but the two personnel had walked back to the tail. I suspected that some damage had been sustained – perhaps to the elevator tip – so I quickly left the plane and investigated. The two refuellers were together trying desperately to straighten the barrel of one of the twin Browning turret machine guns, which they had obviously struck and bent while carelessly driving around the tail section. Both guns were subsequently removed from the turret and replaced. The offenders were placed on charges and a new directive for all refuellers was issued.

Later, there was another dangerous situation when a corporal fitter and I were detailed to check out a hydraulic malfunction with the bomb doors of a Wellington. The aircraft had just been loaded with target bombs, but the bomb doors had failed to close and remained in the half-open position. We were checking the problem when a voice from the front hatch called out, 'Can I come in? I'd like to look around your kite.'

I was in the centre section at the time and answered, 'No, keep out; the plane is all bombed up. Don't touch anything.' The man answered, 'OK. I'll just take a quick look and won't bother you.' So saying, he climbed up the short ladder into the entry hatch, which is adjacent to the bomb aimer's glass rectangular panel, with the bomb release 'tit' on the immediate right. I again ordered him to leave the aircraft.

I could see that he was a sergeant air gunner. He stood, head and shoulders inside the plane, fiddling with something, when suddenly I heard the entire bomb load fall to the ground. He must have found, and pressed, the bomb release. He immediately left the aircraft and, as we quickly followed him, jumped on a bicycle and pedalled away.

The bomb doors, being fortunately in the half-open position, had caused the bombs to turn slightly as they fouled them all hitting the ground on their fins, preventing them from exploding. I noted this as we ran for cover. Miraculously, nothing happened – just blessed silence – and the twenty or so bombs just lay there, all with buckled fins. Our flight sergeant arrived quickly on his cycle, and as we reported the whole incident he said, 'Yes, I saw him race away as I came up.'

A court martial followed, resulting in the air gunner being dismissed from the service. Apparently he had already been in trouble and this was the last straw – and so very nearly ours also!

Occasionally an aircraft fitter would accompany a pilot who was flight-testing a plane after service. Parachutes were mandatory. I vividly recall a test flight when one engine failed and the other began to falter. The pilot and I were alone in the aircraft and he ordered me to prepare to bail out as we were losing height. I opened the main hatch and had my legs over the edge. We were quite low over Bredon Hill in the Vale of Evesham. Looking down onto the snow-covered hills, I saw three figures – one in red riding a black horse. They were waving at us. I remember thinking that if I jumped then, my chute would barely have time to open. The faltering engine suddenly picked up and we lifted away from the hill. The pilot called, 'Get in; we'll make it back.' And we did – another near miss.

On a similar flight that winter, we flew into thick fog. For about ten minutes the pilot climbed to get above it, then suddenly we emerged into a clear sky, but with barrage balloons all around us, sticking up out of the dense fog layer like a field of black poppies. The pilot skilfully made his way out of danger, but it was a close call. Missing the balloon cables was just pure luck.

On another occasion, the pilot said he would fly over a girlfriend's country house. With the house in his sights, he flew around low before a final pass up the long tree-lined drive, clipping the top branch of a high tree as we approached. The flight ended successfully, but inspecting the starboard wing tip when we landed, I found a foot-long broken branch still embedded in the aileron. I consider that a near miss too, but all ended well.

In June 1942 I was posted to the Middle East – with two weeks' embarkation leave. Before my departure, Ted and I managed to enjoy a few days together, roaming the fields and getting in a little fishing. But all too soon the day for departure arrived and, after emotional farewells from the rest of the family, Dad saw me off on the bus for Doncaster, from where I caught my train to Southampton. His final words as he helped me with my kit bag were 'Keep your chin up, lad'.

As the Mediterranean was under Axis control, we left Southampton with destroyer escort and sailed out into the Atlantic. We paid a brief visit to Freetown on the western coast of Africa but did not go ashore, remaining anchored a half-mile out while equipment was offloaded. I asked why we stayed offshore and was advised that mosquitoes would be a problem if we were any closer, and malaria was rife there.

We shortly upped anchor and sailed for Cape

Town, where supplies were loaded, but again we were not allowed shore leave. I remember the impressive Table Mountain on the horizon beyond the city.

A day later we sailed for Durban where, to our great relief, we received permission to leave ship during daylight hours for the next three days. We were given a welcome party at the town hall, followed by a dance and rickshaw tours around Durban. The rickshaws, gaily decorated with African motifs, were pulled by giants who, I was told, were Zulus – most dramatic and memorable, two passengers per vehicle.

After our short stay in Durban we sailed for Egypt, passing through the Mozambique Channel, where we had a submarine alert. Shortly after, one of our naval escorts destroyed a sea mine. However, no further alerts occurred and we entered the Red Sea intact. Arriving at Port Said, we were disembarked and loaded onto waiting transport. A large oil fire was burning near the docks during these few hours, but we were quickly on our way. There was a contingent of army personnel – part of the ultimately victorious 8th Army.

It was 15 June 1942. Our small RAF group of about eighty men was transported to Fayid airport, south of Cairo, which was a well-established peace-time airfield with good aircraft hangars and sealed runways. We also had reasonable accommodation, and we were cheered by these familiar signs of a well-run, secure airfield – it was indeed just that, with at least two other squadrons operating out of it. Visits to Shaftoe's cinema in the nearest town were a frequent treat, with countless delicious egg rolls at the intermission. I was detailed to a newly formed Australian Halifax squadron, No. 462, comprising around nine aircraft. All had been flown direct from 10 and 76 squadrons in the UK to form 462 Squadron.

In the cockpit of Minnie the Moocher, Fayid, Egypt.

I commenced my duties immediately, after medical checks and various inoculations now that we were in a malaria zone, and a couple of days later was allocated to the ground crew of Halifax 'M', with 'Minnie the Moocher' painted on the side of the aircraft's nose area. Operations were continuous, and we were all very busy from that first day, but enemy activity was slight, thankfully. We new arrivals got along very well with the Australians who made up 60 per cent of the squadron personnel. We found them to be relaxed, very good tradesmen and extremely dependable at all times – right through the long months I served with this squadron.

One day in late October 1942, army personnel arrived at my plane and advised us they were placing two five-gallon jerry cans of petrol under the sand in a designated spot near our sand bag protection area. This was to be used to destroy the plane if it was unable to be flown out and the enemy broke through El Alamein to Egypt. Fortunately, this never happened, and two weeks later, after El Alamein and the Axis retreat, the squadron moved up into Cyrenaica.

But prior to this I was detailed, with another fitter and two electricians, to travel up into Palestine, to the RAF base at Akir, to inspect for serviceability the large overload fuel tanks that enabled our Halifaxes to make the flight from England non-stop. These were stored at Akir for possible future use. After a briefing, we were issued with a Sten gun, rations, a few five-gallon tins of petrol, and water – all stowed in a 15cwt light-covered tray truck. Off we went up along the Suez Canal and crossed over into the Sinai to make the halfway house, as it was called, for our first stop. The road was in fair condition and we arrived at the halfway point in the early evening – being escorted the last mile by a dozen mounted

Arabs, all armed. Upon arrival, we checked out the small building, but found it unguarded and of no use to us, so we decided to stay and sleep in our vehicle. We lit a fire to boil the billy and warmed up some tinned food.

The Arabs, meanwhile, had dismounted and were gathered around us just watching and conversing together quietly. We offered food to one who appeared to be the leader – a young man of fierce aspect who was heavily armed like the others, but also carried a silver-mounted sword and dagger. He smiled and refused, but accepted a few cigarettes, which he immediately shared with his companions. Having established some rapport, I admired his sword. He half-drew it and invited me to test its edge – which I carefully did and found it razor sharp.

After watching us eat, they suddenly turned, mounted their magnificent horses and, with a wave from the young man, rode away into the desert. The night was clear and very cold as we kept watch in turns, but it passed without incident. Rising early for breakfast, we found the Arab horsemen had returned and were again standing silently around our vehicle. We lit our sand-filled tin after pouring petrol on it, and heated a can of bacon – when the young Arab leader stepped forward and gave us a bag of eggs. Some of these we cooked for our breakfast, after which we packed our gear in the truck and said goodbye to our Arab onlookers, who, with smiles, mounted and rode away.

We continued our journey to Akir without incident and duly reported to the CO. We were directed to the fuel tank building – actually a small hangar – and our sleeping area. We commenced our inspection of the tanks immediately and finished the following evening. Having found the tanks serviceable, that second evening we drove into Tel Aviv for a couple of beers with some RAF airmen at Betty's Bar, where we spent a most enjoyable time.

The third day we left Akir early and returned across the Sinai, half-expecting to see our Arab horsemen, but they did not appear, and we eventually rejoined our squadron.

Living together in close quarters, we discovered that the Australians on 462 Squadron were expert at dealing with dangerous pests. There being no sticks and few stones in the desert, they would crack snakes like a whip! Fortunately, serious snake bites and stings from scorpions were rare. We quickly learnt to shake out garments, and would grip the toe of a boot and, with a few brisk taps against the tent pole, dislodge anything that had crawled in there. Constant vigilance was required and at night the mosquito nets came into use. Even with care, any limb coming to rest against the net would be attacked, leaving one with itchy blisters and the risk of malaria. There was also the danger of deadly desert sores, which were a very real problem if they became infected. A good friend had deep open infections that resulted in his being moved back to the Delta for hospitalisation.

1943 saw the squadron moving up through Cyrenaica. In places the desert was literally covered by the debris of war. We saw many burnt-out German, Italian and British tanks, together with other vehicles, including an occasional aircraft. I spotted several Italian Savoia wrecks, and the odd Stuka.

Having a cuppa with the team of bomb armourers in El Alamein. All were killed in a freak accident.

The 8th Army, with General Montgomery at its head, was pushing Rommel's Afrika Korps steadily out of Libya by the end of the year, and enemy air activity slackened off. Squadron 462 air operations continued unabated, blasting Rommel's retreating army in Libya and later giving damaging attention to critical targets in Italy. In March 1944, 462 ceased to be Australian in constitution and was absorbed by the RAF while still retaining many Australian air crews in its ranks. The Australian ground crews – having been withdrawn over the past few weeks – went back to defend Australia against the Japanese forces that were moving down through the islands of New Guinea. When they reached Java – just a short flight from Darwin – they were repulsed.

A long time before this, Mother had written to me about a cake she had sent for my twenty-first birthday, and I thought it was lost. It was a big surprise, then, when it finally arrived, hopefully as she had described it – thick icing, lots of fruit etc. So with a few pals, including an old school friend, Cedric Eastwood from Hebden Bridge, we opened it up to find that after its long, eventful journey the cake had been reduced to fine crumbs. And there, buried in it, was a gold cardboard key to the door! As the mixture looked edible, we ate it with spoons and still found it delicious. So with beers all round we celebrated my long-gone twenty-first in October 1942, thirteen months late. Letters from home being so few and far between, even the cake crumbs were gratefully received.

I won't give details of the engineering maintenance work that we ground crews carried out. I'm glad to say that we managed to cope with the manifold problems and casualties to the best of our abilities with the limited resources we had in this dry, hostile area. The further away from established air bases we were, the more difficult it became to fully maintain large, sophisticated aircraft. It is to the credit of all concerned that we emerged from the north African campaign as well as we did, with a high degree of success. I am proud of having been part of it and to be able, in this account, to tell something of a few incidents that came our way unbidden, but which now emerge as clear, sharp, memorable moments in a dangerous, hot, dusty, fly- and mosquito-ridden environment – far from cool, green England.

The Arabs in Cyrenaica, and later in the rest of Libya, were well disposed to us and would barter eggs and dates in exchange for our rationed cigarettes. They preferred Craven 'A' to the South African Cape to Cairo brand. We found the Arabs generally to be shrewd, fair and extremely quick on the uptake and, having had recent dealings with German and Italian troops, they were expert negotiators.

In 1943 one of our Halifaxes developed engine failure and ditched in the sea. We heard that the pilot, Warrant Officer Harold Vertican, and six crew men escaped in the emergency rubber dinghy that was carried by every Halifax. The crew survived on emergency rations for eleven days. Finally, seasick and exhausted, they came ashore in Tripolitania where, with the assistance of local Arabs, they made it back to safety behind Allied lines.

Born in Yorkshire, Harold Vertican was educated at Ilkley Grammar School. He was commissioned and awarded the Conspicuous Gallantry Medal for his leadership in this event. Subsequently, he was promoted to flight lieutenant and awarded the DFC.

A little later in the same year one of our Halifaxes was being prepared for operations and there was an accident as it was being loaded up with 500lb bombs. The armourers were using a new type of delay fusing device, which apparently caused one bomb to explode prematurely and the remainder of the bomb load to explode in the following few minutes, thus totally destroying the Halifax and killing all ground crew and armourers, except one.

A light-hearted moment in the Western Desert.

I was working on a repair job at the maintenance tent, together with a few other fitters, and witnessed the whole scene. After the explosion, we all dived to the ground – thinking it was an attack by enemy aircraft. Fragments of bomb casing were falling all around, but it was quickly evident that this was an accident. I saw a senior officer driving a small pick-up vehicle straight towards the inferno – the Halifax was a ball of fire by this time. He paused as another bomb went off – possibly the sixth or seventh – and then took his truck right up to the burning aircraft wreck, leapt out and lifted the wounded survivor into the vehicle, then made for safety with spinning wheels. All this was achieved between bomb bursts – the bravest action I witnessed in my whole north African campaign.

The rescued airman's arms and hands were severely injured. I remember him sitting outside his tent, waiting for transport to the base hospital. I walked over to wish him well and a full recovery, but I never saw him again. He had been an accomplished pianist. Only weeks before the accident, when we'd moved on to the airfield, which had been so recently occupied by Axis airmen, we found a good piano in a corner of a hangar. The entire squadron was assembled there for a few hours and this airman – now so badly injured – had entertained us with his masterly rendition of the *Warsaw Concerto* – a performance I'm sure none of us will ever forget.

Not long after this dreadful accident, the squadron moved further up through the desert – carefully negotiating the many minefields that had been signposted and identified with barbed wire fencing by our army personnel. Once more we passed debris of burnt-out trucks and tanks, with graves everywhere.

Moving along the Via Balbia in Libya, we saw many of the buildings erected by the Italians during their colonisation of the area, some badly bomb damaged but others – deeper in the desert, beyond the escarpment – in good condition. These were generally being used by the Arabs as handy pens for their livestock. It was not unusual to see a well-built white farmhouse building with a number and 'Ente Colonizzazione Libia' painted in large black letters on outside wall. I guessed this was for civil aerial identification by the Italians.

Water continued to be a high priority for us all. We had a water detail, whose responsibility was obtaining safe drinking water from the few surviving water points. Once I went with the bowsers to an oasis, which I imagined would be a shimmering pond under date palms with Arabs and their veiled women drawing water. So much for imagination! We found only an efficient-looking concrete well guarded by a small 8th Army detachment, who assured us the water had been checked recently and was OK. So we filled the bowsers with clear, cold water drawn from about twenty feet down in the well. Our medics also carried out a check just to be sure. However, later in the year, in Libya, I did see a typical Hollywood-style oasis, complete with Arabs, camels, dramatic black tents and date palms, though the women were not visible.

During a quiet stand-down period in 1943 we witnessed an entire tribe of Arabs moving through the airfield. They were travelling west, no doubt to reclaim their former territory in the Libyan desert, which had now been vacated by Germans and Italians. I remember hoping they would not suffer casualties on any of the minefields scattered around. The colourful assembly took two days to pass – camels, horses and families all laden with baggage and moving silently, almost in single file, the best way to walk through a mined area. After the second day they were gone from our lives and we were left with the empty desert and our Halifaxes – the Arab caravan was just another of the desert's mysteries, which we continued to encounter as long as we were in that strange, remote land.

We often listened in to BBC broadcasts – particularly enjoying songs such as 'The White Cliffs of Dover' and many others sung by the ever-popular Vera Lynn. German radio broadcasts of 'Lili Marlene' were also picked up.

During this brief quiet period a friend and I explored the escarpment that rose about four miles away from the coastal area we occupied. We reached the escarpment cliff face without incident, noticing that a recent heavy rain storm had caused mini land-slides in places. We came suddenly to an area where an entire section of the cliff face had fallen away to reveal a massive piece of Roman architecture, with superb marble slabs engraved with elaborate Latin inscriptions. This appeared to be the end of a noble building deeply embedded in the face of the escarp-ment. I immediately thought, 'Wow, what would an archaeologist think about this lot?' Arabs had already begun to dig under one corner of the edifice and one ran away as we approached.

Time was running out for us, but fortunately I had my small sketch book, so I carefully made a sketch of the exposed building and copied as many of the splendid inscriptions as possible. Even though I was untrained in drawing, I had a natural gift and would sketch everything that inspired me. Eventually we left, intending to return with the squadron commander and a photographer if possible, as I felt this was a major archaeological find that must have been covered since the Roman occupation of the area 2,000 years before.

It was fortunate we didn't stay at the site longer – when we arrived back in camp we found all the tents down and packed onto transport, with our Halifaxes taxiing out and taking off one after another. It was a scramble to find our gear and a place on the trucks.

The sudden move had caught most personnel by surprise. By mid-afternoon we were on our way to Benghazi and well beyond. It was goodbye to the Roman ruins forever, as we never returned.

A few weeks later some of us ground crew were posted to Blida, a large airfield in Algeria not far from Algiers. The Axis had now been driven out of north Africa and were fighting a retreat in Italy at Cassino. During the move to Algiers, we lost a lot of our personal kit, the sea transport having been sunk by a mine en route. We, fortunately, had travelled by land. I lost one of the two kit bags I owned, and this contained my few souvenirs, the letters I'd received from home and also my sketch pad. The one kit bag that survived contained a worn set of pants and battle dress, together with other well-used gear – all coated with soggy goo from a box of soap powder sent out months before by my dear mother.

A letter I received from Ted was even more welcome than usual after all this. During my absence, he'd become friendly with John Wholey, a slightly older student who was in Olwyn's class at the grammar school. John's father was head gardener of Crookhill Estate, which had a fine pond well stocked with perch and pike where the two boys spent many happy hours at weekends. Ted told me about their fishing there and said, 'That was where I could think uninterrupted and where my poetry began to develop, almost like the slow development of a religion.' That pond inspired his poem 'Pike', which begins:

> Pike, three inches long, perfect
> Pike in all parts, green tigering the gold.
> Killers from the egg: the malevolent aged grin.
> They dance on the surface among the flies.

Many others had their origins there too. In his letter he also included his observations of the wildlife of the estate. This was like a tonic for me, surrounded as I was by the vast sands of Libya, with its scarce trees and not a song bird in sight, only hawks. Ted and John's friendship was to last all their lives.

With comrades outside their tent, Western Desert, 1942.

My new posting at Blida was to an RAF Stirling squadron. Our camp was situated on the edge of the aircraft dispersal zone, and alongside an enormous vineyard, full of the most delicious black grapes I've ever tasted – but watched over by an Arab with a shotgun, who sat on top of a ten-foot-high observation platform under a small awning. We were never without large containers of grapes for the entire season. We were also able to purchase good wine from his small establishment near town. In the evenings occasionally we played classical records on our wind-up gramophone. Mozart's 'Eine kleine Nachtmusik' was a great favourite with our group and the occupants of the surrounding tents.

Operating from Blida and located alongside us was a USA squadron of Flying Fortress aircraft. I remember that the US elections were in full swing, and their airmen paraded camels adorned with the slogan 'Vote for Ike'. Eisenhower did very well in the election! We liaised amicably with all the American personnel and many friendships were made in the few weeks we operated side by side at Blida. The Americans were extremely competent on all levels and I missed them when I was posted to Boufarik a little later.

The Yanks, forever busy and doing interesting things, had obtained a popular French small aircraft, a single-seater called the 'Flying Flea', and often during quiet periods would take off in the Flea and buzz around the airfield. One day when it was passing overhead we heard the motor stuttering, then silence, and down came the miniscule Flea at a steep angle – right among our dispersed four-engined aircraft. The pilot, however, skilfully brought the Flea in, missing the assembled aircraft to finish gently under the wing tip of a Stirling. That was the last time I saw the Flea on our airfield.

During our time there, we were disturbed through the night by the howling of a large pack of dogs on the move through the suburbs. The French locals explained that these were domestic dogs gone feral and the local pack, one of several, lived in the nearby mountains, which lay about ten miles beyond Blida. These packs frequently swept down through the neighbourhoods searching for food, and God help any chickens or sheep that were not safely locked away at night. My pals and I occasionally visited Blida and were quite apprehensive about these wild dogs. When going into town, we each carried a part of a dismantled Sten gun just as insurance in the event of meeting a dog pack – or whatever!

Late in 1944, I and some others were posted to Boufarik, a small town about twenty-five miles from Blida. The personnel were all senior fitters. As we arrived, our tents were being erected by German prisoners, who came to us twice a week from a large

POW camp in Algiers. They were an interesting lot, being drawn from the air force, navy and Rommel's Afrika Korps, and all appeared to be resigned to their captivity without any visible evidence of stress.

The prisoners would line up for inspection by their sergeant, in his Afrika Korps uniform. This sergeant would often ask me to correct his English. As a result, we had many discussions, with my German acquiring a Hamburg accent, while his English had a distinct Yorkshire flavour!

On 5 May 1945 our CO arranged a game of basketball with a nearby Canadian Army detachment, and we played on the excellent school sports ground in town. All went well until I fell after a tackle, fractured my left wrist and had to be sent for treatment in Algiers Hospital. VE Day had just been announced – 8 May – and the day after my wrist was plastered about thirty Allied personnel currently being treated in the hospital were invited to a party to celebrate. The party was held on the lawn in front of the hospital, with nurses and doctors joining in on what was a very happy occasion indeed!

After my fractured wrist healed, I returned to Boufarik to find all work on our Spitfires had ceased and the factory area was being cleared of equipment. During this period, 48-hour passes were issued, regularly enabling me and pals, one of whom was Hugh Hughes, to spend time with civilian friends we had made – particularly in Pointe Pescade, a lovely seaside resort near Algiers, where we had over the past few weeks enjoyed swimming trips arranged by our unit. Hugh especially appreciated this period of light duties, since he had met and proposed to a lovely French girl named Simone. They eventually married and enjoyed a long and loving relationship.

Another bonus that came our way while awaiting transport back to England was that we found the Paris Opera Company was in Algiers, having been evacuated from France when the Germans moved in. A few of us managed to see several of the classic operas presented in the fine Algiers Opera House before our final departure.

I saw my precious gauges and tools loaded for the military disposal depot in Algiers and we then proceeded to the south coast of Italy, where we found welcome temporary accommodation. This interlude gave us ample opportunities for sightseeing in Sorrento, and particularly in ancient Pompeii, where pre-war excavations had uncovered intact a large Roman town, buried beneath volcanic ash and lava. At the time of our visit, the public were not permitted entry, but our small RAF group was allowed in for four hours before the gate was locked again.

I remember seeing some of the many bodies of the citizens of Pompeii caught in the eruption of Vesuvius in AD 79. They were lying in the dwelling of a well-to-do person, with colourful murals of aspects of the town's life depicted on the four walls around them, the floor made of fine tiles with a mosaic motif at the door. The human remains, coated with hardened white ash, were perfectly preserved, some crouching, covering their heads with their hands, one in the act of running from that awful deluge of hot ash. Two large dogs – guard dogs by their size – were also caught in mid-stride, perfectly intact.

It was a dramatic scene, from the ruined temples to the street of whorehouses preserved just as they were 2,000 years ago, with carved stone male genitalia displayed above each entrance, leading to a solid, stone-walled room ten feet square with a single stone bed. Most of all I recall the body of a tall man, where the concrete-like ash had broken away from his outstretched foot revealing a sturdy sandal with the buckle and curled strap – just as the owner had pulled it on all those centuries ago. That sandal said it all for me – the whole tragic story, a glimpse of the past that is totally unforgettable.

Meanwhile, back in our temporary accommodation, transport home was still unavailable, but with so much of interest nearby we filled these remaining days very easily. We visited a monastery in Sorrento, where we were surprised to see well-stocked shops. I purchased silk stockings and shoes for my mother and sister and a wallet for Ted. For Dad, I found a very fine leather belt.

At each of our pauses in the journey, military police (Red Caps) checked us over for weapons taken as souvenirs, and I witnessed a few very interesting objects being surrendered en route. Before boarding ship, we passed in line before the duty officer with MPs standing by and a clear notice advising all troops to hand over non-issue weapons, otherwise any forthcoming leave entitlements would be jeopardised. On the table in front of the seated officer was a pile of twenty or so German and Italian pistols. This careful check was repeated upon our disembarkation at Dover, prior to the ship docking. Many weapons were discreetly dropped in the water.

The Channel was calm, and our voyage without incident. As we slowly entered Dover harbour, there was a boy of about ten sitting on a box, fishing. He was the only civilian to greet us back with a cheery wave, and with that friendly gesture we knew we were safely back home.

Chapter Six

Home Sweet Home

When I returned home to Mexborough, the door was opened by Ted – now a tall, good-looking young man. He just stared, with tears streaming down his face, and in a strong voice said, 'Mam, it's him, it's him!' It was September 1945. I was twenty-five and Ted was fifteen years of age.

Ted outside Dad's Mexborough newsagents, 1946.

After a big hug, he picked up my kit bags and we went into the house to be met by my mother and father and my sister Olwyn. What a reunion we had – one of the best days of my life. We all sat around our large table and, as I answered their eager questions, I emptied my kit bag of the many presents purchased from the shops in Sorrento.

My family had survived the difficult war years very well. Olwyn told me how Eric, the son of our Mytholmroyd neighbour Gertie Barker, who had become a prosperous caterer and food shop owner in Hebden Bridge, often drove forty miles to see them and keep them well supplied. She particularly recalled a seven-pound pot of Yorkshire clover honey that she and Ted devoured! Food was still rationed, but quickly improving, and all were noticeably relieved that the stress of possible invasion and the bombing blitz were now past and life could be lived again as in the pre-war days – a 'beginning again' feeling prevailed.

Ted and Olwyn were still at Mexborough Grammar School and their studies were well advanced. They had new friends and ambitions. In due course, Olwyn went to London University – she had won both a state and county scholarship and had opted for the state one – and Ted to Cambridge. Indeed, I wondered how I was going to fit back into a family that was ticking over so comfortably.

Me with Mam while on embarkation leave, Mexborough, 1941.

I was still in the RAF and on a month's leave while awaiting my next posting, so I tried to relax with the family and enjoy the new post-war England. I even managed to get in a few days' fishing in the big pond at Crookhill with Ted and John Wholey. The weather was good and though we caught a few perch, the big pike that was said to be there eluded us.

Ted questioned me endlessly about my experiences in Africa, and it didn't surprise me that in due course he decided to do his national service before taking his place at Cambridge, following me into the Royal Air Force. As youngsters, of course, we had spent many happy hours together making and flying model planes, so the interest was there from an early age. Naturally, Ted's air force experiences were far duller than mine

– after all, fortunately, it was peacetime not war – but he made good use of the time, shutting himself away when he could, reading all of Shakespeare's plays. He was also writing a great deal, already determined to be a poet, and filling the notebook he always carried, honing his talent.

But that was still a couple of years in the future. Back in Mexborough, where I found myself once again, nothing had changed. It was still a coal-dusted, grim place, the miners continuing to call in for their cigarettes, which were in short supply, and Mam and Dad's shop was busier than ever. But after the desert's expanse, it felt to me to be a small, crowded town. Ted and I visited our relations in Mytholmroyd to find that Uncle Walter Farrar had lost his son James to pneumonia. Granny Hughes and Uncle Albert had also died, and Ted and I affectionately recalled how, on our hunting trips, thanks to Albert's influence and the Wild West stories and accounts of the Red Indian wars he introduced us to, we had generally assumed the romantic character of Indian hunters after wild game.

However, my remaining uncles and aunts were all in reasonable health. The few years since our leaving Mytholmroyd suddenly seemed like a lifetime ago. I was only twenty-five, but felt more like forty-five, so much had changed and been lost. It was all like a dream – a feeling that stayed with me throughout my entire leave. I loved every minute of it, but never felt that Mexborough was a place where I could settle down and live.

My Spartan existence in North Africa had caused me to lose weight. Mother said I looked a bit gaunt and badly in need of feeding up. I also had a problem with external lip blisters, which the RAF medical officer said indicated a mild dose of malaria, though he nevertheless cleared me of the disease. The blisters reappeared every August, but disappeared largely after 1949. I still have them occasionally – in August!

It was inevitable that in my absence my family had changed, society had changed, but I also had changed, and it was not a comforting thought. I had a sense of impermanence. That is what the tensions of war and travel had done to me. So although I went through the motions of getting back some of the life I had lost, an inner voice was quietly reminding me that this was only a temporary state, to enjoy while I could, for my life was going to go in a new direction. I found out soon enough how things were going to change for me when my much-needed, restful leave came to an end and a new posting arrived, with instructions to report to a RAF base near London.

So there were more goodbyes. I took a train for London, where I joined a small group of RAF aircraft fitters. We were briefed for our next move, which was, after a medical and overnight rest, to board a DC-3 aircraft – destination Almaza airport, Cairo, where further instructions would be given us.

As we took off, London and the lovely English countryside was folded away behind us and I quietly thought, 'Well, here I go again, but the war's over, what lies ahead for us now?' We landed at Gibraltar for refuelling and a meal, then headed for Cairo, across the Mediterranean, en route for the north African coast. We safely flew over two convoys of around thirty ships each, which were no doubt loaded with armed forces returning from the now quiet battle zones around this so recently dangerous area.

We made landfall directly over the Roman ruins of Cyrene – flying in low, which gave us a good view of the extraordinary remains located a hundred yards from the quietly lapping edge of the sea. These ruins are in stark contrast to the vast surrounding desert.

I thought about the place's past – the industry and art and the thousands of voyages made by Roman galleys laden with all the requirements of the ancient city. I also thought of the garrison needed to protect this asset of the Roman Empire. I had read of the flow of African wild animals conveyed by galleys to supply arenas throughout the length and breadth of this great empire for many hundreds of years, until the fall of Rome in AD 475. Cyrene and Carthage – not too far away – had opened Africa up to the Romans.

We set course for Cairo, over the Via Balbia

highway leading to Egypt across Cyrenaica, passing El Alamein, where in 1942 the 8th Army turned back Rommel's Afrika Korps, and so on to our destination. The date was August 1945. On arrival, we were allocated tents near the main hangar, where several DC-3 aircraft awaited our attention.

While in Egypt, we fitters would occasionally accompany the pilot test-flying the plane after a major or minor inspection or component change. On one such flight we were returning when I heard the warning horn that indicated the undercarriage should be in the 'down' position. I looked out and saw that the airfield was coming up, the runway was directly ahead, and we were too low to have the undercarriage still up. I realised that we had a problem and hurried forward to the cockpit where the pilot was on his own. He wasn't paying any attention to the horn, but was staring fixedly ahead. I touched his shoulder and pointed to the undercarriage lever. He just nodded in a dazed way, so I promptly selected 'undercarriage down'.

We continued our descent unchanged. The gear seemed to take ages to lock down, but the green light eventually came on, the horn ceased its clamour and almost immediately the wheels touched down – a fairly heavy landing, but a safe one. I was still standing beside the pilot as he was taxiing in and parking the aircraft. He then told me he was ill with a fever and thanked me for the timely help, but it was one more near miss!

The city of Cairo had not changed much since my earlier visit in 1942. I noticed an increase in the numbers of army personnel taking in the sights while in transit. The sense of urgency had gone, with its accompanying tension.

How fortunate we all were to be there with the war over. I gave thought to the thousands of our comrades and enemy personnel who were gone, and would remain in their silent grave sites – from El Alamein in the vast desert, up through the length of Italy, and every corner of Europe – forever.

After a few weeks, the workload tapered off, and our group flew back to England. I was immediately posted to RAF Thornaby – an Air-Sea Rescue squadron in the north of England – where, to my surprise, I was promoted to corporal, with two years' back pay. The paymaster, I remember, queried the length of the back-dated promotion, saying, 'Well done, you've certainly been around, but don't spend it all at once.' The Thornaby squadron flew mainly Wellington aircraft, so I found myself working on the plane with which I had begun my RAF service.

On 12 May 1946 the day for my demobilisation came, together with a promise of further promotion in the near future were I to sign on for a few years.

However, I was feeling like a change from service life, and so I was duly demobbed at Thornaby.

Returning home on the train that day after a few farewell drinks in the squadron canteen, one of my pals proclaimed, 'No more polishing brass buttons for me,' and he wound down the window and threw all his cleaning kit out to underline firmly the finality of his service life. I, being a Yorkshireman, took mine home – waste not, want not! Predictably, Mother asked me to use it the next day – to polish a brass camel Dad had brought back from the First World War.

I was looking around for interesting work and saw in the newspaper that the Nottingham City Police Force was looking for recruits. I applied, was accepted, and commenced a training course in August 1947 at No. 3 District Police Training Centre, No. 18 Recruit Course. After several weeks' excellent training, I passed the final exams and found myself in the Central Division of the Nottingham City Police.

Nottingham is an attractive city, with its splendid castle and many fine old buildings. My work consisted mainly of week-long shifts, with the first week 6 a.m. to 2 p.m., second week 2 p.m. to 10 p.m., and third week 10 p.m. to 6 a.m. Patrols were the norm, and an occasional stint of traffic point duty. I enjoyed police work, but good accommodation was hard to find, and throughout my months of service I changed mine four times, each time for similar reasons: small room; no – or at best minimal – heating, making it hard to dry off one's uniform adequately from shift to shift; and poor food generally – except in the good headquarters canteen.

My sergeant made a comment one day to the effect that a wife, a warm, dry home and good meals were an absolute essential in the police force. I didn't have a wife, and certainly no warm, dry room to return to after a cold, and often wet, eight-hour shift.

Meeting an inspector one dreary, rainy, early morning while on patrol, the inspector addressed me with 'Carry on, officer' then, as he got back into the police car he turned and said, 'Cheer up, Hughes, the first ten years are the worst.' I thought that he was probably right, and when I returned to my chilly room, in my damp uniform, I decided that he was definitely right! So, what exactly could I do about it?

That problem was solved most effectively just a few days later. I was returning to headquarters in falling snow, with my thoughts on the cheerless lodgings and my usual struggle to dry out my uniform waiting for me, when my attention was drawn to a large sign in a travel agent's window that read, 'Come to the sun: migrate to Australia.'

So in I went, and within ten minutes was signed up to migrate to the sun, as the advertisement said. My comrades in the Australian squadron in north Africa had highly recommended their country many times in my years with them. The travel agent suggested that I resign from the force very soon, saying, 'You'll be on your way within four or five months.'

Back at headquarters I discussed my decision with my sergeant, who approved the move. He had close relations in Australia who were very happy there and loved the weather and the life. I was still on probation, which required a two-month notice of my intention to resign. But this gave me ample time to adjust to the imminent big change in my life and to say my goodbyes to my friends in the force. Of course, I had to break the news to my family at home and start planning for my move to Australia.

This waiting period also gave time for reflection and the serious consideration of what was involved in migration to a country on the opposite side of the world. Ted was in favour right from the start, which eased many of my little worries. He was keen to achieve a degree at Cambridge, after which he would join me in Australia. In the event, his plans changed after meeting the American poet Sylvia Plath. Ted's parting gift to me was a complete works of William Shakespeare.

In December 1948 I joined a group on a ship called the *Esperance Bay*, due to sail to Australia that month, and so it was that I departed England's shores again, but this time to begin a new life down under. After approximately six weeks we made landfall at Fremantle in Western Australia, with all the passengers crowding the rails to see the emerging continent. The distant shore slowly came into focus, with a Londoner, in a broad Cockney accent, drawing attention to an enormous smoke cloud, 'Cor, Blimey, we've come 14,000 ruddy miles and the place is on fire!'

When I arrived in Melbourne, Victoria, I was met by a Mrs May Batterby and her family – old friends of my father's. She was a widow who had moved to Australia years earlier to live in Sandringham, where I was given a warm welcome. From there, I found employment with Australian National Airlines (ANA) as an aircraft mechanic, based on my RAF service experience. I needed to find room and board nearby, and to my good fortune found accommodation with the Whelan family. Not only was this comfortable, but it had an added attraction – the Whelans' lovely daughter Joan. When I first met her, she was frantically involved with a large social set, almost ignoring my presence as I studied for, and obtained, an aircraft engineer's licence for DC-3 aircraft, and six months later for DC-4s. Somehow I shyly asked her out on a simple date. Gradually we became ever closer and married in 1950. Her wonderful parents helped us obtain a bank loan for a deposit on land to build a home.

My interest in painting was reignited in 1950 – my second year in Australia – when, having seen some remarkable paintings in the Melbourne Art Gallery by a Mr Hans Heysen (later to be knighted), whose studio was in Hahndorf, South Australia, I decided to try to make his acquaintance.

I did not own a car at that time, but a friend I worked with had a small, box-like Austin 7. The friend was Allan Betteridge, who was continually recounting the major overhaul he was engaged in with his car. This week was kingpins; last week was the cylinder head and valves, and so on. We both had two weeks' leave coming up later in the year, so when Allan said that he was satisfied with the car and invited me to make a road test trip, I accepted. We agreed to drive up to New South Wales and to check out the duck shooting on the rice farms. We could then drive along the Murray Valley Highway into South Australia and call on Hans Heysen, hoping to find him at home. If this plan failed, we could pay a visit to one of Allan's relations in Adelaide.

So, each of us being around 6'2" in height, we squeezed into the Austin one day late in the year and took off for our trip – my first real look at the Aussie countryside. Allan drove, while I just sat, taking in the dramatic rural scenes unfolding – so very different to England.

From our starting point in Essendon (a Melbourne suburb), we made for Echuca, just on the Victorian side of the river Murray, which we followed along the

Murray Valley Highway to Swan Hill – seeing only two mountain ducks by the side of the road. While pausing for a meal outside Kerang, I spoke to a local farmer, saying we had hoped to find lots of wild ducks, but had seen only two. He smiled and pointed to a long, dark cloud a few miles away, explaining that the 'cloud' was actually ducks who were being disturbed and moving around some crop where they would descend again to feed.

Etching of an early settlers' farm, Pambula, NSW.

We continued our journey through Swan Hill, seeing many kangaroos and emus on the way, with flocks of white cockatoos, rosella parrots and galahs coming in to drink along the river.

Crossing into South Australia, we eventually arrived at

Ted and Carol
with Uncle
Walter, 1973.

Ted writing home at 'Coolyarren' during his visit to us in Australia, March 1976.

ABOVE Ted and a teenage
Nicky, target practice
at Moortown Farm,
Winkleigh, Devon.

LEFT Ted landing his catch
on a Devon river.

During his fishing trip with Nick in Kenya, 1983 – Ted with 'the big one', his Nile perch, 104lbs.

LEFT Olwyn and Ted in London, 1978.
MIDDLE Carrying on the family tradition of cycling – Nick at home in full gear.
RIGHT Ted and Horus at the Temple of Edfu in Egypt, November 1984.

ABOVE Ted and Carol,
leaving for a Farms for City
Children event at Iddesleigh,
April 1986.

LEFT Learning the art in the
Bodega, Jerez, 1986.

Ted with Joan and me and
the head chef outside the
Kinnaird, 1990.

Joan joins Ted and me during our fishing trip on the river Tay, the main event of
our Scotland trip, 1990.

LEFT Meeting Ted in Scotland after twelve years, 1990.
RIGHT Ted and Carol leaving Court Green to give the Queen Mother her birthday poem, August 1990.

Ted surveying pastoral Devon, summer 1990.

Ted and our Aunt Hilda amidst the daffodils of Court Green.

Finally tasting that Laureate sherry, which arrived at Court Green some years after Ted selected it in Jerez.

Ted with the artist Leonard Baskin at Court Green, among the daffodils in front of Ted's writing hut, April 1998.

LEFT Frieda posing on our Mornington home's deck in the early 1990s during her Australian visit.

BELOW Ted and Carol 'meditating' with the Queen Mother, May 1998.
© Lady Penn

Aunt Hilda and Frieda at The Gables, Halifax, Yorkshire, October 1999.

Hahndorf and were directed to The Cedars, the home of Hans Heysen. As we entered the drive, I noticed a car and trailer caravan parked behind the house, but no one in sight. We walked around the large dwelling and knocked on a door. I heard footsteps and the door was opened by a slim man of approximately seventy years with white hair and a rosy complexion. He wore German-type knickerbocker trousers and a cardigan. He didn't seem perturbed by two strangers, but regarded us calmly and asked what he could do for us.

I introduced Allan and myself, explaining briefly who we were, and said that we would like to meet Hans Heysen, the artist, having admired his work in the Melbourne Art Gallery. He said, 'I am he, and you like my work? Which paintings particularly?' He did not emerge from the house, but stood back, appraising us carefully.

I began by saying that I particularly liked a large oil painting labelled 'Pomp of the Departing Day'. He said he was pleased to hear that the gallery had brought that one out of hiding and asked which others I admired, so I gave him details of others and where they were hung in the gallery. He then moved forward, saying, 'Forgive my caution, gentlemen, you really do know my work.' Indicating his car, he said that he was about to depart on a painting trip up into the Flinders Ranges, but considering our interest and that we'd come such a long distance, he could give us an hour. This was all he could spare, unfortunately. He invited us into his studio, which lay about eighty yards behind the main house, up a slight incline, and was surrounded by a few impressive gum trees. He asked whether either of us painted. Allan said that he didn't, but that I did.

Homemade plough on the settlers' farm.

Inside the studio, which had a large, deep fireplace, he showed us a part-finished watercolour standing on an easel and several paintings by other artists hanging on the walls. I considered it to be a very comfortable place in which to spend time painting and relaxing.

There was a large bucket of water standing on the floor and Mr Heysen spoke of the importance of using clean brushes, stating that nothing would diminish the light and life of a watercolour more than the use of a carelessly cleaned brush. Another tip he gave was that

when painting a natural scene in a wood, it is important to pay particular attention to the side detail, the
peeling bark, broken branch stumps and so on. There
is an enormous amount to register on such a painting
before giving detail to the front of the tree. Then with
the attention that's been given to the sides, the painter
can establish the tree's character. All this requires a
great deal of skill.

My final memory of this most interesting man, later
to be acknowledged as one of the great painters of the
Australian bushland, was when leaving his studio, he
paused and drew our attention to an enormous gum
tree, commenting on the wonderful colouring of the
branches glowing in the sunlight. I felt I was seeing
them for the first time, and have admired them in a
special way ever since. His last words to us were, 'Have
a safe journey home, and good painting for the future.'

I never saw Hans Heysen again, but this magical
interlude has stayed with me, as I am sure it has with
Allan, influencing my painting and appreciation of
the fascinating Australian landscape.

After returning to Melbourne, I commenced
evening art classes at Swinbourne Technical School,
followed by a year at the Melbourne Kew studio of
Allan Martyn – a fine local artist. Since then, my
painting has settled into a lifelong hobby.

Part III

Keeping in Touch

Dear Gerald + Joan, thanks for the
…t letter + drawings. I like the drawings very
…ch — the Candlestick Tree the two
…les, the tangle of T Trees or whatever they
, the grave going down to the sea, and
plant like a bonfire. All very interesting
attractive pieces.
You sound not too rooted in your new
…mpost. after [illegible] the blister-hot
…alls of your [illegible] once I wondered
…aw you could stay solid going farther north, where
Australia is there a reliable shadow? Then
maybe you'll relax + begin to love Ocean Parade
I'm off in a couple of days to Alaska —
…r 3 weeks with Nicholas. We shall drift do…
river from the big lake at the top — about a
…eek or more. In the lake we shall try to catch
the Trout +, Nicky's speciality, burbot — which
…are delicious eating. In the top of the river we
shall catch big Grayling — the fish Nicky is
…rshipping in his thesis — and biggish Rainbow tro…
… dry flies + nymphs. A little lower down we
…all be meeting the Sockeye Salmon + maybe
…aps not very likely some steelhead — big sea-r…
…ainbows strongest of all those fish for their size.
Finally we shall come to the first battalions of
Kings — the big ones. They go up to 50 lbs
that river — occasional 60 — mostly 30-4…
half way down the river to a little place called
… used to be a couple of old timers

One of Ted's many letters.

Chapter Seven

Cambridge and Ted

I was missing the family, so for Christmas 1951 my wife and I decided to visit England, mainly for Joan to meet my family in Yorkshire. Mam and Dad had by now sold the business in Mexborough and bought a new home, Woodlands, in Todmorden – just a few miles from our old home in Mytholmroyd. It was quite the nicest house they ever owned – a spacious, well-built, terraced Edwardian building on the edge of a golf course. But there was a steep trek down to the shops and Mother never really liked Todmorden, especially as her rheumatism – about which she never complained – took hold.

Ted had won an open exhibition to read English at Pembroke College, Cambridge, while my sister Olwyn was already at London University, studying English at Queen Mary College, and both were home for the holiday.

It was a wonderful reunion for us all, with cold, snowy weather. One day Ted produced a steel bow and said, 'Let's have a bit of target practice,' so off we went to a nearby field and I quickly found that he was as skilled with his bow as he was with a rifle.

Ted, the archer, Todmorden, 1952.

Other days we drove around Mytholmroyd visiting relations and old friends, and I gave Ted some driving lessons, which led to his getting a full licence at a later date. He greatly enjoyed these outings, which gave him a break from his studies. One special day, we took Mother across the moors to a remote and lovely area where we managed to bag several grouse. Ted wrote a poem about that day, 'Anthem for Doomed Youth', which is to be found in his book *Wolf-Watching*. In the same book, you'll find 'Dust as We Are' for our 'post-war' father William, imagining Dad's experiences in the trenches. Ted once said, 'Poetry is a way of contacting your family when they are gone.'

Examples of this are the two elegiac poems included in this book, 'For the Duration' and 'Anniversary', written after our parents' deaths, and 'Brother Peartree', which I've also included later.

Joan and I stayed in England for some ten months, taking a flat in Streatham. Since we were newly married and not exactly flush, we both found jobs – Joan working as a secretary for Lawfers Chemical Company in Regent Street, and me as a ground engineer with BEA (British European Airways). It was my aircraft engineer licence from Australia, valid for DC-3 and DC-4 aircraft, that helped me get the job.

Having finished his national service and now at Cambridge, Ted was able to come down to our flat most weekends – they were very happy days. As there was still food rationing in England, we were delighted to receive a large food hamper from Joan's parents in Australia. Joan made a large batch of Neenish tarts, an Australian delicacy, which Ted – lean and hungry as usual – swooped on gleefully, declaring, 'It's like eating jewels!', a name that we gave those tarts from that day on. We drank white wine and a lot of coffee, and talked endlessly. Ted continued to visit us whenever he could and we had a few outings to local dances. Ted, being a fair dancer, greatly enjoyed these.

Joan and I had purchased a second-hand Austin, and one weekend we all drove down to the White Cliffs of Dover; on another we returned with Ted to

Cambridge. We booked Joan into a hotel and then Ted took me to his rooms in Pembroke College, which is on Trumpington Street and one of the oldest Cambridge colleges. Dating back to the fourteenth century, it has a beautiful chapel by Sir Christopher Wren.

Ted and Joan under the White Cliffs of Dover, 1952.

So I briefly entered the enchanting world of Cambridge, Ted showing me round proudly before we went up to his rooms at the top of the stairwell. There I was particularly struck by a startling black-and-white sketch he'd done on the wall of a jaguar in short perspective. We talked for hours, Ted filling me in on his life there. He was writing poetry intensely at that time and clearly found his room and the whole Cambridge ambience a magnetic and conducive atmosphere in which to write. But he was also proud of the fact that whenever he had to rustle up a quick meal, fellow students would smell the appetising odours and converge on his room, staying to chat and exchange views. He was also, as you would imagine, very popular with the ladies.

Ted outside the gates of Pembroke College, Cambridge, 1952.

Just as we were about to retire for the night, Ted switched on his radio and we heard on the news that the temperature that evening would drop below freezing point. I suddenly remembered that my old Austin was parked outside the college gates with no antifreeze in the radiator and that the gates were locked. When I explained to Ted that it was now too late to drain the radiator, he enthusiastically offered to climb over the college wall, but I dissuaded him. Fortunately the car started the next morning and we were able to drive off without any problems, heartened to have found Ted in such jovial form.

Ted and Joan at the Roman baths, 1952.

Joan and I also went on a trip to Bath with Ted, who had a growing interest in archaeology. He was particularly captivated by the original part of the baths. He'd been fascinated by my wartime tales of the ruins we'd come across in the Libyan desert and had marvelled at the Romans' skill in the planning and construction of their temples and villas in a barren area where there were no suitable materials. He was greatly taken by the thought that they must have been conceived and manufactured in Italy and then transported. 'Just imagine the planning and skilled labour necessary,' he exclaimed. 'And the loading onto galleys and the building and architects required.' It fired Ted's imagination and curiosity and he vowed to study this period in Roman history in more detail.

From Bath we drove on to Wales, where we quickly found a suitable camping area for our Bukta Wanderlust tent, but as it was pretty cold we decided to sleep in our warm, dry car in the end. It wasn't as comfortable as we would have liked, but we finally got to sleep – only to be awakened by a sharp tapping on the window. I lowered it cautiously to reveal a farmer, who said we would sleep better in his barn.

He asked where we were from, and when Joan said Australia he exclaimed, 'Oh, then you live in the bush, oh my goodness, you will freeze to death in the car.' However, being dry and firmly ensconced, we thanked the farmer for his friendly offer and decided to stay where we were, though in truth we would have been better off in his barn!

All in all the Wales trip was a great success and a fitting finale to our stay. We returned home in good shape, but broke!

We'd planned to spend ten months in England and before we knew it ten months were up. It was hard leaving the family, but we vowed to keep in close touch – and that we did, exchanging letters frequently. After we had returned from the visit we started on our first family home – 224 Lancefield Road, Tullamarine (near to Essendon in a newly developed area). A close friend recommended an architect, who designed an impressive four-bedroom residence, which was actually two houses joined together by a connecting hall. It turned out to be fortunate that our new home was on the large side, for it soon needed to accommodate our young family – in 1954 our first son, Ashley, was born, followed by our second son, Brendon, in 1956 – as well as Joan's mother, Gladys, and father, Maurice, who still suffered pain from shrapnel wounds received at Gallipoli during his service in the 4th Light Horseman Division in the First World War.

By then I had secured a good, steady job as a sales rep with an agricultural engineering company. Joan joined a law firm in the city as a legal secretary and, with the help of her mother, managed to go on working full time, while at the same time fulfilling her domestic roles as a wife and mother to our two young sons. We were both very involved with their education and many hobbies.

Fortunately for us, Ted was a great letter writer. He still had serious intentions of joining us in Australia and had even applied for a visa. He saw it as a 'paradise' – doubtless from what we had told him. He planned to get a teaching diploma on leaving Cambridge so that he would not starve once he came, although he saw teaching as a kind of compromise.

He wrote to us in August 1953 to keep us up to date with the news. Olwyn, he told us, was working in Paris, our parents were fine, he was contemplating cycling down the west coast of France with a friend, was penniless, and had painted green-and-red leopards down one wall of his room.

He'd also decided to put new curtains up, so he'd measured the various windows and sent the measurements off to Mam, who'd agreed to sew them up for him 'to smarten the room up a bit'. Ted had asked for a nice, gentle green colour, but when the curtains finally arrived they were black and all the wrong size. 'All they are fit for,' Ted wrote to us, 'is to blindfold elephants.' Knowing how meticulous Mam was and her skill when it came to sewing, I suspect Ted's measurements may have been wrong – in metric, perhaps, rather than feet and inches.

Ted seemed to be relishing his time at Cambridge – working, singing, drawing – getting up at 2.30 in the morning to work, then going back to bed at 7 a.m. and sleeping for a couple of hours. 'By this means,' he told us, 'I get two sleeps and am as fresh as a flower.' He felt it was like living two lives. He also wrote to me about his piano playing, which he'd taken up and which he said 'comes on very slowly'. He spent a lot of his time reading folklore, which had captivated him from an early age, and the poetry of Yeats – and listening to Beethoven.

For all this, he seemed to have an ambivalence towards the university, which was revealed in a letter he wrote to Olwyn: 'Sometimes I think Cambridge is wonderful. At others, a ditch full of clear, clear water where all the frogs have died. It's a bird without feathers; a purse without money; an old, dry apple. All the gutters run pure claret. There's something in the air, I think, which makes people very awake.'

Perhaps it was that he'd grown really dissatisfied with his chosen subject – in a letter to me written shortly after our visit he announced that he had changed his course from English to archaeology and anthropology, and now he was learning 'all about the beginning of life and everything since'. Upbeat and interested as always in others, he then turned his attentions to my wife Joan, who he believed had a real literary talent. Light-heartedly he suggested they should go into business together, with him inventing plots and Joan writing the stories, 'to their mutual profit'. Flattering indeed, but it never came to anything.

Chapter Eight

Sylvia

Ted was convinced from an early age that he was going to be a poet, but meeting Sylvia Plath in 1956 intensified his ambitions – and called a halt to his already well-formulated plans to join us in Australia. As he wrote to Olwyn, 'I have met a first rate American poetess. She really is good. Certainly one of the best female poets I ever read and a damned sight better than the run of good male ... for the last month I have lived about the strangest life I ever did live.'

Within four months of meeting Sylvia in Cambridge at a party to launch the magazine *St Botolph's Review*, in which Ted had four poems, they were married. I learnt about their impulsive wedding from Ted, whose letter was quickly followed by one from my parents, telling me that he'd brought Sylvia to meet them and how lovely and intelligent they found her.

From the letters Ted sent me at that time, it is clear just how intoxicated Ted was with Sylvia and she with him. 'Marriage is my medium,' he wrote. 'You have

Sylvia, photographed by Ted during their 1957 USA trip...

...and Ted, photographed by Sylvia!

no idea what a happy life Sylvia and I lead.' Sylvia had already sold and published her poems in the US and had begun to make a name for herself, and though Ted had published a few poems at Cambridge and afterwards, he had not yet reached that stage of recognition. They worked together closely, reading and criticising each other's works.

Regrettably, I never met Sylvia, but she and Ted wrote to me frequently and at length, so through our letters I was able to keep in close touch with them during their years together, as they were with me, and we felt close. Apart from their letters, they phoned from time to time, describing their plans, thoughts, ambitions and travels.

Ted, not surprisingly, had retained his love of fishing – I'd given him a large, green rod before I left for Australia and though it took a long time, he did eventually manage to get Sylvia to go fishing with him. However, I don't think it ever excited her as it did him, though Ted said she loved it and had 'luck'. She certainly shared his intense appreciation of the natural world. 'We walk out into the country and sit for hours watching things. We sit by the river and watch water-voles and when they come near, Sylvia goes almost unconscious with delight.'

From wherever he and Sylvia lived or travelled in the few years before their children were born and they settled in Devon, Ted wrote me detailed letters.

From Wellesley in Massachusetts, where they went in June 1957 to meet Sylvia's family, travelling through what seemed to Ted like Red Indian country, he wrote about the blackbirds with vivid red flashes on their shoulder, robins 'as big as thrushes', jays, fireflies and skunks. Although appreciating the warmth of their hospitality, Ted was clearly overwhelmed by his new American family, the apparent opulence, the social rounds. 'I'm going to get some fishing tackle,' he wrote, 'and keep myself buried as deep in what these 85-foot-long Cadillacs cannot reach.'

From there, it was on to Cape Cod, where Sylvia's mother had rented a cottage for them as a wedding present (Ted called it a kind of 'dowry') and where they planned to have time to themselves and to write. At first, though, Ted found the cost of the place – $70 a week – inhibiting, even though he wasn't footing the bill. Cape Cod, he wrote pithily, was a place where 'the folks bring their families, or businessmen bring other men's wives'.

There was a 'black week' when Sylvia fell into a deep depression and Ted developed a huge abscess on his ear. Fortunately a doctor was found who gave Ted the necessary antibiotics and his ear cleared, as did Sylvia's mood. They began to write like 'angels', Ted actually penning one children's story a day before breakfast. According to Ted, everyone in the area hunted and fished and drove about loaded with armour and fishing permits, boozing heavily. On Cape Cod, evidently, the deer season lasted only seven days and Ted amusingly reported that during the last season 'seven deer were shot and seven deer-shooters'.

Like Ted, Sylvia seemed to enjoy writing us long and descriptive letters, and although, as I said earlier, we'd never met – largely because my job had kept me busy – I began to feel as though I had.

A colourful Christmas card from Sylvia and Ted – sent from Northampton, Massachusetts, where Sylvia was teaching at Smith College – brought in the New Year of 1958:

Two stags leaving gold footprints and a gold sky of snowflakes to say our Merry Christmas to you. My teaching tends to take up most of my time so far – keeping a week ahead of my seventy girls like a fox eluding the panting hounds ... Manage to cook a lot now, though, which I love – so Ted and I regale fellow writers and teachers on wine or tea, casseroles, and spaghetti sups, pineapple upside down cakes – my one main way of being creative, unless making up classes on D. H. Lawrence and Dostoevsky could be called remotely that. But come June 1st I'll be writing again at last, trying to finish my own first book of poems this summer and begin some stories. After a short, dry spell, Ted is producing poems prolifically again and we hope to live and write in Boston next year, away from this grove of academe.

Ted added his own note, his thoughts turning to our two-year-old son Brendon, as he urged me to 'recite and recite to him. Then when he grows up he'll have the means to express himself in his head and won't have to start learning ten years too late.'

By the time Ted and Sylvia reached Boston in August 1958, a town Ted found 'very pleasant, very gay', he was in a philosophical mood, again display-ing his concern about the educational development of our children and a wish to see them. Over the years he would send us children's books, urging us to read them to Ashley and Brendon and to tell them stories separately so that they, in turn, could then tell them to each other, thus developing their vocabulary and imaginations. He reflected: 'The most vital factor in a child's education is the life its parents lead. You make your own life and you make your children's with it.' He added: 'We are writing children's books at present – it would be pleasant to try them out on your pair.'

In that letter he also brought up the idea of my coming to England and running a farm with him, a notion he had floated several times before. He clearly saw this as a way of achieving some kind of financial independence. (Earlier he'd come up with the fanciful scheme of having a mink farm.) To that end, he was familiarising himself through magazines with the state of farming in England and seemed intent on pursuing this, even if I wouldn't. Of course, now that we had a family, moving back to England was not really an option for us – just as Ted's coming to live in Australia with Sylvia was not really an option for him. 'Australia is too far from Rome, Paris, Madrid and the Mediterranean coast for us to think of that,' he wrote.

In May 1959 we received a very upbeat letter from Sylvia, outlining their plans for the summer:

> We plan to take a camping trip this summer, borrowing my mother's car, to California and Mexico, through all the big national parks. I am very excited about this, and so is Ted, as we've never seen anything west of New York. Then we will go for September and October to this castle artist's colony in New York State where we have both been invited to spend two free months writing. I won't have to shop or cook, which will be a wonderful change, although I'll probably be dying for a homemade cheesecake or fish chowder after a week. We plan to write up all our summer experiences there, then sail for England some time in the winter.

She goes on:

> Ted & I have both finished writing books of verse for children & are hoping to sell them here. His is called

'Meet My Folks', 8 very funny rhymes about a zany family … My ambition at this point is to get a story in the New Yorker. They have taken two more poems, so this year I have earned over $500 from them, for only 4 poems, which is rare pay.

She wrote affectionately about Ted, too, saying he was thriving and more handsome than ever. She had, she wrote, just bought him a red-and-black woollen sweater, in which he looked 'marvellous'. 'If he has any faults,' she continued, 'they are not shutting the ice box (a kind of subconscious revenge on American appliances) and knotting his clothes up in unknottable balls and hurling them about the floor of the room every evening before retiring. Oh yes, and the occasional black moods when he pretends the cat's ear is broken or that the air is full of Strontium 90. Other than these minor foibles he is extremely good-natured, thoughtful and almost normal.'

She ended that warm and graphic letter by urging us to send pictures of the children and to write again soon.

As planned, that summer Ted and Sylvia were off on a tour of the West, the incredible space and wildness of the prairies reminding Ted of the Yorkshire Moors – though they were full of grass and crops instead of heather and there were no valleys. He was clearly excited by the fact that they were about a hundred miles north of Custer's Last Stand and near other famous battlegrounds – and no wonder, given his childhood love of Westerns. 'I think we will stay and try and see the buffalo,' he wrote.

It was in the very beautiful Yellowstone National Park in Wyoming, which they visited in July 1959 during a ten-day tour of the area, that they had exciting encounters with bears that roamed the camp. The animals paraded themselves quite openly – sometimes with their cubs – sniffing round the rubbish bins at night, looking for food. Ted reported having seen sixty-seven bears in all; one of them – number fifty-eight – actually tore the side window of their car out with its claws in the middle of the night, lifting out Sylvia's red handbag and opening a tin of biscuits. One unwary woman had evidently been killed, and on hearing this Ted and Sylvia moved further away from the trash cans. Quite an adventure. Ted found the fishing in the area 'incredible'.

Chapter Nine

Two of a Kind

Ted was hankering after a return to England,
where he now had a growing reputation following the publication of his first book, *The Hawk in the
Rain*. Apart from his literary life, he clearly missed his
family and wrote regularly to our parents – urging
me also to do the same and give them lots of news.
Sensitive as always, he told me, 'When you write,
make sure you include Dad in your audience. He
doesn't write, I know, but he's very hurt if the letter's
directed to Ma, and in answering her letters one
tends to write to her only. But she's writing for him.
Don't forget.'

Ted and Sylvia, who was now pregnant, left
America in December 1959 on the *Queen Elizabeth* and
arrived back in time to join our family for Christmas.
How we would have loved to have been there.

With the birth of their daughter Frieda imminent,
Ted and Sylvia were glad to find a flat near Regent's
Park in London, tiny though it was. It was a wonderful

spring for Ted – his first book winning the Somerset Maugham Award and his second volume of poems, *Lupercal,* winning the Hawthornden Prize. This book also received a rave review from the influential critic A. Alvarez in *The Observer.* As always, we received copies, signed and with a warm note included, with cryptic comments on the poems. For Ted and Sylvia, the arrival of Frieda, born on 1 April 1960, set the seal on a perfect homecoming.

Ted and Sylvia returning to England on the Queen Elizabeth, *1957.*

From Sylvia, a little while later, came a joyous account of Frieda's early months, included with a letter from Ted ('Ted had already sealed up your letter in his secretive way, but I made him open it again to let me gossip for a bit'):

The baby is so funny – singing, making faces, cuffing her teddy bears, giggling at our oafish attempts to amuse her. I put her on 3 meals a day at 5 months, so feel to have acres of time now that the 6.10.2.6.10 schedule is over. She eats like a pig. Following after her ma. Her eyes are an astounding blue, which neither of us gave her: she gets it from her two grandfathers. Already little boys hang about her carriage acting up for a smile. Every time I leave her to go inside a shop I find somebody or other kootchy-kooing over her and she looks out at everybody and is very curious.

This afternoon I took her on one of my favourite walks in Regent's Park by the Scotchman's Zoo – where you can see a lot of animals without having to pay to go in. I attracted a large white camel from the zoo-goers at the opposite side of the outdoor cage by making sly squeaking noises and got the camel bending over Frieda's carriage eating grass from my hand: she was amazed and amused. I think she thought it was Ted in an overcoat.

Her letter was not all delightful baby talk and included reference to a play Ted had expressed self-doubts about in his letter: 'Don't believe a word Ted says about his one-act play,' she wrote. 'The play is superb ... full of brilliant, colourful, *speakable* poetry. Some of the scenes are killingly funny.'

Clearly her mind, like Ted's, was back in the literary world and her letter concludes: 'We popped out for a couple of hours to a literary cocktail party in posh Kensington – at John Lehmann's, editor of *The London Magazine*. He's a regular publisher of our stuff. So we cultivate him ... Lehmann was serving champagne ... and I managed with my usual sleight-of-hand to enjoy a good bit of it. ... Frieda says 'ba!' which means she sends her love. So do I.'

That Christmas, Ted and Sylvia took Frieda to spend the holiday with my parents at The Beacon in Heptonstall, the house they had moved into after selling Woodlands in the mid-1950s. The Beacon was not as large, a 1930s building with a small garden giving onto fields, fine views of countryside and shops near at hand in Heptonstall village. It was walking country – on the 'tops' Mam loved, though increasing rheumatism kept her fairly close to home. Evidently, as space was at a premium, my parents had sold the piano on which we had learnt as children to make room for Frieda's playpen. A few months later – in March 1961 – my mother wrote me a long and

revealing letter that included an account of that visit.
Here, in part, is what Mam wrote:

Dearest Gerald, Joan & Ashley & Brendon,

I can't tell you how Dad and I look forward to
your precious letters. I'm afraid I have been lax in
writing ... It was lovely to hear about the two little
chaps going off to school all spick and span with their
new schoolbags. How I would love to see them. Do
you remember going to Mytholm school, Gerald?
I can remember holding your firm little hand and
waving to you as you turned up the lane to school...

I had a letter from Sylvia this morning. She is in
hospital in St Pancras, London, not far from home.
She has had her appendix removed, but she seems
now well on the road to recovery and very well satisfied with the hospital ... One gets the best of attention
under the Welfare State. Sylvia's operation and
treatment will cost her nothing. She said Ted visited
regularly and last weekend he wheeled Frieda in her
pram to visit her and she was allowed to sit up in the
hospital garden with them. She hadn't seen Frieda for
nearly a week, so you can tell what a pleasure that
would be for her...

She and Ted broadcast together in a program
called 'Two of a kind' ... Well, it was lovely ... Ted
broadcasts a lot, I wish you could hear him. In the
'Two of a kind' he told how, in answer to a young

man who questioned them, he started learning about birds and animals from you, Gerald, and how you both used to go up on the moors shooting ... Then Sylvia told how they met at a poetry party in Cambridge, about their courtship during which he had saved some money while working in London as a script reader for Rank Studios ... It all sounded very light-hearted and then they told how they lived near London Zoo and that they had a little daughter who was wonderful. Everybody who heard them said how lovely it was. Ted had also broadcast to schools on poetry and he talked last Saturday evening after the news on 'Learning to Think', in which he said he did not learn to think at school, he learnt while relaxed and quiet as he sat fishing on the banks of a pond.

You asked, Gerald, if he has changed. No, not at all, he is quiet and rather wistful and likes a funny joke. Of course, he always was fairly quiet, wasn't he. Sylvia is strong-willed but I think left alone they are very happy together, if you know what I mean. She is very possessive and I think she resented Olwyn and Ted's close affection for each other. It was a pity because at times one felt the strain, and not least Ted. But on the whole they get on well together, not as lively and cheery as you and Joan. You always seem to have sunshine around you. Sylvia and Ted seem more sober. Of course, her father was German, you know, which perhaps accounts for it and her extreme thoroughness in her work. I used to long to pick Frieda up and nurse her – we had a playpen for her – but Sylvia used to say 'Don't nurse her, or I won't be able to work when I get home.' So back in the pen went Frieda Rebecca with her lovely blue eyes and head shaped just like Ted's when he was small. Funnily, Olwyn remembered and remarked on that too. She was as strong as a little horse and stood up with the railings of the pen as nice and steady as could be. Sylvia's mother is arriving from America in June so we will see her...

Dad has just had his tea, sausages and mash potatoes, and is now asleep with his hands clasped on his tummy. He looks well and is not too fat.

Everything you sent us at Christmas has been lovely and very much appreciated. Olwyn really enjoyed her visit home. I wish she was married and settled, though I can't really pressure her. She is very smart and looked well and is very amusing. After Ted and Sylvia had gone back to London we used to stay up talking until 3 and 4 o'clock in the morning. Dad would go to bed early, Ted and Sylvia always go fairly early, so we didn't stay up late then so as not to disturb their rest. But time seemed so precious as Olwyn only comes once a year. I wish you could have been here too ... She is very sensible and has a good job and is not short of money anymore.

Ted and Sylvia had wanted to get away from the intensity of literary London life, and in 1961 they bought Court Green in Devon.

In a 1986 letter to the poet Anne Stevenson, who was writing *Bitter Fame*, a biography of Sylvia Plath, Ted explained:

> You should know how we ended up in Devon, rather than somewhere else. Your remarks suggest that you suppose we went there because I liked the rural life. In those days, all I wanted was circumstances in which I could write and follow my own schemes, and not be forced by financial demands into some job. Sylvia too was sacrificing a lot simply to see what she could do if she did nothing but write for a few years. So Devon was partly, almost mainly, the flight from the heavy financial demands of living in a city. Our idea was to mobilise what talents we had, for living off our wits, until we could afford to take next steps.

They were both, in Sylvia's words, 'wild' about the place. It was, she wrote, 'Ted's big dream' and they'd bought it from a Sir Robert Arundel. According to Sylvia, Ted nearly didn't go for it 'because for some reason he is prejudiced against titles and we only saw it for fun because of it having a thatch … of course it was enchanting, made us fall in love with it – it's white with a black base-border and this bird-haunted straw top.'

Although it had six bedrooms, they were going to have to camp out for a year, Sylvia told us, because they had no furniture or carpets and a long list of repairs, 'such as tearing up the floor in two front rooms downstairs and getting them cemented ... and then replastering all the rooms.'

They both said they would miss London, but they clearly hoped to get a lot of writing done to pay for it all and for the education of their children, 'of which', wrote Sylvia, 'we're due another in January'. It was heart-warming to sense and share their happiness and their joy about the house and about Frieda, 'a blue-eyed, brown-haired doll, very funny and full of jokes, and loving, kisses her toys and jabberwocks at them ... She is our great toy and keeps us in charming tempers.'

Mam, Ted and Sylvia with baby Frieda in Yorkshire.

In the midst of all this they found time to urge me to send them some of my paintings, which they were sure they could find buyers for in London. Even more than ever, painting had become my great passion, and Ted particularly continued to be both complimentary and encouraging about my work, which I would send him from time to time over the years. That meant a great deal.

In another note, sent around Christmas time, Sylvia wrote:

> We are undergoing genuine Christmas weather – yesterday, driving back from Plymouth, where Ted did a BBC broadcast, we shopped for a rug to cover some of our acres of as yet bare boards … The first snow blew down on us and it was awe-inspiring driving back over the dark reaches of Dartmoor. Hail this morning – then everything clear again. I miss my crisp, white, six-foot American blizzards – we used to have such fun sledging and building igloos. I suppose I'll be telling Frieda about 'the old days in the old country' where everything was just slightly legendary.

She said they were gradually getting Court Green into shape. Ted was painting the ghastly upstairs floorboards, which were making them feel like 'ill-kept horses in a barn'. The following spring they planned to tackle the front room downstairs and the garden too, and when spring came she wrote again to say that she had been happily browsing in the 'dirt of our lovely vegetable garden'. Ted was evidently a marvellous planter, but she said he did not see weeds. However, it seemed she did, pulling out gigantic nettles, dock leaves and dandelions.

'I love it here and so does Ted. He looks wonderful, very happy and is able to be relatively unbothered by his famousness, which hounds him in London.' She had, she informed us, received an American grant to finish a novel, so they felt confident that they would 'weather the first year of giant bills and tax inspectors'.

Chapter Ten

Break-up

After all the upbeat and happy letters and occasional phone calls we received from Ted and Sylvia, as well as from other members of the family, it was naturally extremely upsetting to hear about Ted and Sylvia's separation in the autumn of 1962.

I'd expressed our concern in a letter to Olwyn, and Ted wrote me a heartfelt letter from our parents' home. In it he expressed his great admiration for Sylvia ('in many ways the most gifted and capable and admirable woman I've ever met'). He went on to explain that the break-up was finally, in some ways, a relief. 'All this business has been terrible – especially for Sylvia – but it was inevitable.'

Despite this, all our hopes had been that they would somehow get back together and resume a relatively normal family life with their very young children. So the dreadful news of Sylvia's suicide in February 1963, which we learnt about from my parents, was a terrible shock – all the more so since, at that time, we had little knowledge of Sylvia's emotional struggles. Of course, we could not then have read her journals, with their record of her fears and terrible nightmares, nor were we aware of her earlier suicide attempt when a student at Smith College.

Sylvia's loss made us feel closer than ever to Ted and our family – even though we were at different ends of the world – as happens when sad times come. We looked for a way to come to England to see them all. Ted and my parents had never met our children, nor we his. At that time, though, my job as a rep for an Australian company made it impossible to leave Australia.

It was 1964 before I finally managed the trip. I went first to see Mam and Dad in Yorkshire, then to Court Green. Olwyn had come over from Paris in September 1963 to help with the children until Ted sorted things out. She expected to stay a month or two but ended up staying for two years, until October 1965.

A sketch of Court Green with St Peter's church in the background.

During that time, after a four-year job in Paris with theatre agents, and with Ted's encouragement, Olwyn started her own literary agency, initially handling Ted, Jean Rhys, who lived nearby, and the poet Robert Nye. She also translated a French novel for the publisher Andre Deutsch while in Devon.

It was sad that my first visit to Court Green, which Sylvia had described so enthusiastically, should be after her demise. It was, indeed, as she had written, a lovely, well-proportioned house, led into by a wide expanse of lawn in the front and rows of apple trees. Idyllic.

It was during this visit that Ted talked to me about Sylvia's suicide and the events leading up to it. Only now, when we were able to talk frankly and at length, did I come to realise how profoundly it had affected him. Ted was always a very private man and such discussion of personal affairs did not come easily to him. Her death and the circumstances surrounding it continued to haunt him, and I found him in a poor state, mentally and physically: he complained of feeling unwell, which was very unlike him. Dad, too, was in a terrible state, and my mother's ill health only contributed to the general mood.

From Ted, among other things, I heard how Sylvia had become more and more worried, even paranoid, about her work, particularly her forthcoming and deeply personal book *The Bell Jar* – how it would be received and whether it would sell. Her nervousness about its content made her decide to publish it under a pseudonym, for reasons that would later become clear. Again and again Ted had tried to reassure her, but her anxieties grew, and the emotional tension between them and the increasing marital strains reached an unbearable pitch. The situation was inflamed by Sylvia's awareness that Ted had become infatuated with another woman, Assia Wevill.

Sylvia insisted that Ted move out and he complied, going to stay in London. At the time he hoped and believed it would be a temporary arrangement, thinking that being separated from him would give Sylvia space to deal with the emotional turmoil she was going through – and that he too would have time and calm in which to refocus and to work. He kept in constant touch with Sylvia and the children, visiting Court Green, and when Sylvia decided she didn't want to spend the long winter alone in Devon, he helped her with the money to lease a London flat.

He continued to see them regularly, and although Sylvia talked of divorce, Ted baulked at this, believing they could get back together. He missed the children terribly, and he missed Sylvia. In one sense he was right about giving her space, since it was during this period that she wrote her most famous poems. However, as she feared, *The Bell Jar* appeared to indifferent notices and the launch – which Ted attended – was rather low-key.

Ted told me how panicky he had become about Sylvia's mental state as the months went by, and particularly about her reliance on certain medication she had been prescribed by an American doctor, which could make her vulnerable to suicidal tendencies. He worried that she might be taking this medication alongside that prescribed by her British doctors – as indeed she was – and that a combination of the two might be lethal.

It was a painful conversation, Ted talking passionately about the circumstances surrounding Sylvia's actual suicide,` the failure of someone to get there in time, the fact that he believed she had wanted to be rescued.

He was clearly still in a fragile state. After Sylvia's death he had put Court Green on the market, and in fact had a buyer, but the buyer wanted to have a chicken farm in the grounds and the council refused permission, so the sale fell through. At the same time Ted had attempted to buy Lumb Bank Manor, near our parents' home in Heptonstall, but he finally had to stay in Court Green. I know Ted desperately wanted me to bring the family over and move back to England and that his attempts to buy a large residence in Heptonstall were partly prompted by this desire, but I could still not consider returning to England with my young family.

Nevertheless, I relished my reunion with Ted and

resolved to return to England, with my wife and family this time, as soon as possible.

By late 1966 I was in Devon again – Frieda was now about six and a half and Nicholas about four and a half. By then, Ted was living with Assia Wevill and their daughter Shura. They had first met when Ted was with Sylvia and Assia with her husband, the poet David Wevill. Assia, a strangely beautiful woman, had been born in Germany, but her parents had fled to Palestine when she was six – her mother was a Christian, but her father, a respected doctor in Berlin, was Jewish. She had an exotic quality and was artistic, which Ted appreciated. I recall little Shura listening while Ted read children's stories to Frieda and Nicholas, very much part of the family.

A playhouse for Frieda and Nicholas had been built by our father – their grandfather Bill – and he also constructed a writing hut for Ted in the south-east corner of the garden where he could write in peace.

Nicholas was an adventurous and boisterous lad. He would charge round the room pretending to be a rhinoceros, butting people, snorting and shouting, 'I'm a rhino!' Frieda was already quite lovely and she would follow Ted and me as we strolled through the fields, talking animatedly. Ted was always at pains to point things out to her, and perhaps that's when she started to develop her own eye as the very talented painter and poet she was to become. She baked a batch of scones for us and I remember her taking them carefully out of the oven while we watched nervously. They were slightly overdone, but we enjoyed them just the same.

In early 1968 I wrote to Ted saying that we were planning a trip for the following autumn. He wrote back at once. 'Great news. Yes, you can all squeeze in here. By then I shall have other rooms anyway – so there'll still be room to spare. Ma and Pa are very excited.' Ted was particularly pleased that Peter Brook was directing his adaptation of Seneca's *Oedipus*, which was to star Sir John Gielgud, about whom Ted confessed some doubts – 'wonderful man though he is, he is incapable of acting the demon, or speaking like a stone age witch doctor.' He ended his letter with a plea: 'Send some eagle's feet (very important).'

Regarding Ted's odd request for eagle's feet, this is perhaps the place to mention that over the years Ted made a number of such strange demands, and we complied as best we could. Eventually we sent not only those feet, but a tiger's claw, mounted in gold, which we bought when visiting India, and Joan sent him a hat and gloves made from leopard skin, also from India. I also posted Ted a very large python skin to add to his exotic collection. Ted later wrote asking for a dozen kangaroo pelts, tanned, nice and soft, which he intended to have made into a special coat. Amusingly, I learnt only recently that when Ted went on a poetry reading tour to Israel with four other poets, he had difficulty convincing the British customs officials that the five-inch tiger tooth he had with him – a present for his friend, the Israeli poet Yehuda Amichai – was just that!

We arrived in England with Ashley, Brendon and Joan's mother Gladys in December 1968. First we went to Court Green, where we stayed for three days, spending a white Christmas and meeting Carol Orchard, whom Ted was to marry in August 1970, two years later. Carol bought presents for the children and spent some time with us. She was training as a nurse in the hospital in Exeter where our mother had spent time during her illness.

Very attractive and slightly on the shy side then, Carol was genuinely down to earth and would have a stabilising effect on Ted. She was certainly most warm and welcoming to us, and I always remember how readily our children took to her, as did we. In the years that followed – they were to be married for twenty-eight years – she was to bring calm and order to Ted's life, his chaotic schedules and his emotionally taxing work on many levels. It was an awesome role to fill.

From snowy Devon, joined by Ted and the children, we proceeded to Yorkshire, where Joan and I stayed with my parents at The Beacon and the boys with our relatives, David and Rita Farrar and their family, nearby. I relished showing the children the area in which Ted, Olwyn and I had grown up, introducing them to Dad and other members of the family. Ted and I drove to Mexborough with Nicholas and visited the Crookhill pond where we used to fish for that elusive pike. The lodge was a ruin and the pond had – in Ted's words – 'shrunk to an oily puddle about twenty feet across in a black basin of mud'. Ted's name was carved on the trees. He made one token cast – what he called 'a ceremonial farewell' – and to his amazement hooked a huge perch. It was very weird; as Ted put it, 'a complete dream'.

We did a great deal of sightseeing on that trip – from Buckingham Palace to Stonehenge – as well as taking in all the villages and towns around our Yorkshire home.

The year 1969 proved to be a very black one for Ted. Assia, with whom Ted was still involved, had returned to London with Shura late in 1967. Ted continued to visit them often. He and Assia had spent a few days around Manchester, where he had a reading, looking at houses. He described them as 'dreary places down sodden drives' and nothing ever came of it. Tragically, in March Assia took her own life and that of little Shura. Ted was shattered. Then, less than two months later, our dear mother died. Poor Mam had suffered bouts of debilitating chest infections and heart problems, which led to periods in hospital, where she passed away on 13 May. Ted, anxious for our father Bill's wellbeing, moved him down to Court Green. During the summer Ted finally bought Lumb Bank in Heptonstall (which he had first attempted to acquire in 1963) and moved there in September.

Our mother Edith is beautifully recalled by Ted in his poem 'Anniversary', which I'm glad to include here. She was such an inspiration and example to all three of her children, and I have always found Ted's poem deeply affecting.

Anniversary

My mother in her feathers of flame
Grows taller. Every May Thirteenth
I see her with her sister Miriam. I lift
The torn-off diary page where my brother jotted
'Ma died today' – and there they are.
She is now as tall as Miriam.
In the perpetual Sunday morning
Of everlasting, they are strolling together
Listening to the larks
Ringing in their orbits. The work of the cosmos,
Creation and destruction of matter
And of anti-matter
Pulses and flares, shudders and fades
Like the Northern Lights in their feathers.

My mother is telling Miriam
About her life, which was mine. Her voice comes, piping,
Down a deep gorge of woodland echoes:
'This is the water-line, dark on my dress, look,
Where I dragged him from the reservoir.
And that is the horse on which I galloped
Through the brick wall
And out over the heather simply
To bring him a new pen. This is the pen
I laid on the altar. And these
Are the mass marriages of him and his brother
Where I was not once a guest.' Then suddenly
She is scattering the red coals with her fingers
To find where I had fallen
For the third time. She laughs
Helplessly till she weeps. Miriam
Who died at eighteen
Is Madonna-like with pure wonder
To hear of all she missed. Now my mother
Shows her the rosary prayers of unending worry,
Like pairs of shoes, or one dress after another,
'This is the sort of thing,' she is saying,
'I liked to wear best.' And: 'Much of it,
You know, was simply sitting at the window
Watching the horizon. Truly
Wonderful it was, day after day,
Knowing they were somewhere. It still is.
Look.'

And they pause, on the brink
Of the starry dew. They are looking at me.
My mother, darker with her life,
Her Red Indian hair, her skin
So strangely olive and other-worldly,
Miriam now sheer flame beside her.
Their feathers throb softly, iridescent.
My mother's face is glistening
As if she held it into the skyline wind
Looking towards me. I do this for her.

She is using me to tune finer
Her weeping love for my brother, through mine,
As if I were the shadow cast by his approach.

As when I came a mile over fields and walls
Towards her, and found her weeping for him –
Able for all that distance to think me him.

When Ted wrote to me from Court Green in the spring of 1970, he was clearly still in an unsettled, troubled state of mind and longing to have us in England:

Sorry for the long silence … such turbulence over Xmas that I retreated from Yorks. Not at all sure LB was a good idea. Last year was no time to make decisions I'm told … On and off over the last two years I've been looking for a house around Bideford [north Devon]. Suddenly, I found the most staggering property ... 37 acres grazing – sheltered, hilly land, leading right down to the sea, cliff and rocky beach ... So how about it? How about coming in on it? ... You could play with bullocks etc. here – just to keep a bit of income. We could fish. We could sell LB in time and get another place in Ireland. What the hell else are you going to do – you're fifty this year!

In August 1970 Ted married Carol Orchard in London. They spent some of the autumn at Lumb Bank and during that time Joan and I visited them there for a big family meal to mark their marriage. However, it was clear to mc and Carol that Ted was very troubled at this time. As I recall, Frieda and Nicholas had started attending the primary school in Heptonstall that autumn term.

Ted and theatre director Peter Brook, beginning work on Orghast, *Tehran, summer 1971.*

I didn't hear from Ted until the following spring, when he wrote, 'Long silence … This last 6 months has been the bitter end of this last two years … As if my real life had been suspended since the age of sixteen or seventeen.' Ted told me that there was a possibility of his working again with Peter Brook, first of all in Paris and then in Persia, as indeed transpired. After the Persia visit he wrote to me about an extraordinary coincidence:

We were driving down from London, and on a long lovely stretch a mile East of Mere, in Wiltshire, when Carol saw a dead badger at the side of the road. It was hot weather, & already a bit high, but not too bad, and the biggest badger I've ever seen, with a beautiful coat, so I stowed him in the back of the car, intending to get his teeth & bones if not his skin. For one stupid reason and another I left him a day, & was too late to skin him. Two days later, we were going back up to London to collect the kids and take them up to Yorks for the weekend – we wanted to collect some books etc. So on the road, one mile West of Mere, there was a beautiful fox just killed – too badly smashed to skin, but head perfect – so I hid him in the hedge. We were marvelling at this – to see a badger & a fox on two consecutive runs, and I was measuring the distance from the fox to Mere, & from Mere to where we'd found the badger, to see if it was exactly the same distance between each of them

& the town, and when the exact distance came up on the milometer, we were going exactly over the spot where we'd found the badger, and so I said 'It was exactly here', & pointed at the side of the road, and there about three yards off my finger end was another dead badger. This time smaller, & skin not as special. But I hid him in the hedge. Then as we came back down after the weekend I stowed the head of the fox and this other second badger in polythene bags & brought them back.

I imagine the second was mate to the first – probably smelt his death on the road & sat there mourning for two or three nights till a lorry came along & killed her on the same spot. So now they lie together in my ossuary, attended by the head of a fox.

Even now, Ted never really gave up on his hopes that I might one day return to live in England, and particularly his idea that the ideal life for us would be running a farm together: 'We missed getting the very beautiful land all along the river … Mill house for sale in Ireland – write straight back if you want it?' But as I have said this was impossible from my point of view, particularly as I had a responsible job and was now sales manager for a large engineering company.

Land prices in Devon were going through the roof in 1972. In a letter to me in July, Ted wrote, 'Involved lately in panic over property. Just in the middle of negotiating for a mill/farmhouse.' Ted bought three properties, the first a thirteen-acre block on the outskirts of North Tawton; the second a 95-acre block called Moortown; and the third a mill with two acres near Okehampton. Ted brought in Carol's father, Jack Orchard, who'd been a farmer, to run the farm, which he did with great flair.

Ted the farmer with a very newborn calf.

Ted became enthusiastic about the farm, especially after the purchase of their bull in 1974, which he wrote to me about at length – his name was Sexton Hyades the 33rd. At the same time, he lamented the fact that he had been unable to 'unload' some of the cows they had, which he was gradually replacing with pedigree stock. He did manage to persuade Olwyn to pay for a pedigree south Devon female to match his 'phenomenal bull'. Ted was enthralled by the bull, writing, 'This bull is my best purchase ever – I never enjoyed owning anything so much. I really love him. Carol carries photos of him, which we display at every opportunity.' It wasn't, said Ted, just the incredible size and beauty of the animal that attracted him, but its 'strange, sweet nature'.

In that same letter, changing subjects abruptly, he talked about his visit to Buckingham Palace to receive the Gold Medal for Poetry from the Queen. 'She surprised me – very lively and nimble … John Betjeman (Poet Laureate) led me in. Carol, meanwhile, entertained the Keeper of the Privy Purse.' Then, changing subjects once more, he complained that it had been the wettest year in centuries and that the price of hay had risen to twenty pounds a ton.

But the real, moving message of this letter was contained in its opening paragraph, which affected me deeply: 'The final realisation that you will never come and live over here was probably what knocked me out – it was a big station in my life's journey to realise the emptiness of that dream. Part of the general stripping away of everything, lately drastic.'

Over the years Ted continued to express such feelings and regrets, but never, perhaps, more poignantly than in a poem he wrote for me years later, 'Brother

Peartree'. It is a personal message to me on Ted's hopes and regrets at our years of separation: him in England, and me with my family and life in Australia.

Brother Peartree
Yellow and peach pink –
A translucence of late October
Thinner day by day
Reveals what's not there.

I send you fewer letters – fewer and thinner
Year by year. Can I really be thinking
It's just not worth it any more?
What was it I once hoped for?

Paradise. The whole bag of dream
That boyhood was made of
Heavy with rivers and forests. And the game
Quaking the earth like a drum.

Then I made do with a folktale tree
You planted in my orchard.
That's our shared life – that pear-tree.
We're that little in touch.

The year sticks leaves on it – they drop off.
I still stick sentences
On our plans for us –
They drop off.

Pretty yellow and flamey pink.
Till the boughs are an empty crate.
It has never brought me a single pear.
Is it too late?

Or the wrong side of the earth?
Your roots are here, as we say.
Drinking my thoughts. So those branches are roots.
And the real, the flourishing tree

Is on your lawn in Australia. Maybe
The one that ripened for you that gigantic,
Protected, solitary pear
Which you tied with a string to its branch

Just to make double sure –
But you never got it. He did –
Lounging in from your garden, slurping the core,
Your friend's awful kid.

Chapter Eleven

Family Visits

Early in 1976 Ted wrote to say he had accepted an invitation to participate in the Adelaide Arts Festival in South Australia, and he suggested bringing Dad to stay with us for a while. Naturally, we were thrilled. We hadn't seen Ted, or Dad, since our visit to England in 1970. They arrived at our home at midday on 5 March, and Ted's first words were, 'So this is 224 Lancefield Road.' Quite a moment.

Once Ted had phoned Carol to let her know they had arrived safely, we settled down to lunch – Joan's mother Gladys had prepared a sumptuous roast meal. There was a lot of catching up to do, and of course it was very exciting to have Ted and Dad in our home. Ted had lost none of his energy and natural curiosity, and despite the long journey was keen to start looking around as soon as possible. So, once we'd finished eating, I drove him and Dad down to our beach house, which is located on a hill in the Mornington peninsula area. Ted loved it and stretched out in the sitting room, which he felt was a lovely, quiet place where he could write – which indeed he did over the next few days, relaxing in the solitude and privacy, sipping a cold Australian beer. He was fascinated by the stark, bright sunlight and the way it cast long, interesting shadows over the bushy area. One particular aged amber gum tree caught his attention and he peeled off some bark as a keepsake of his visit, while I carved the name of our house, 'Coolyarren', onto a large piece of tea tree wood.

I remember Ted being interested in the presence of a family of wild rabbits that lived close to the beach house, and which I loved to sketch. 'Are there any foxes about?' he asked me. I told him that there were very few, but that what you could see were six-foot-long snake tracks all over. That really caught his imagination!

The family of rabbits that so fascinated Ted.

Another trip we made was to Flinders, on the ocean side. Ted immediately remarked, 'I like your house with the bay view, but this is where you should have built.' Ted was intrigued by the abundant birdlife and questioned me on everything. He was quick to note how different our magpies were from the English long-tailed magpies. He also made me show him some of the many oil and watercolour works I had done over the years, featuring the contrasting Australian countryside, trees and buildings and some favourite fishing spots. He seemed to like the watercolours particularly, and pictures of the dry desert-type areas, which he called the Waste Land.

A sketch of a nesting sparrowhawk, an example of the kind of birdlife Ted and I observed during his visit.

So Ted left us after a short stay to go to Adelaide, but he was much impressed by the Australian way of life and the sunshine, which was such a change from the weather he had left behind in England. The bright warm days continued throughout his stay and the arts festival was a great success for Ted, although he had to endure the heckling of feminists in the audience and accusatory placards about Sylvia Plath's death. It always upset and angered me that such a gentle and caring man should have had that kind of welcome from people who could have had little knowledge of the real and complex circumstances behind Sylvia's tragic demise. He continued his reading, nevertheless, and then flew on to Perth for another reading before returning home to the UK, vowing to return soon.

At the time of Ted's visit, my son Ashley, then in his early twenties, was working as a trainee research assistant for ABC (Australian Broadcasting Commission). Several of his colleagues in the special projects department were in fact covering Ted's tour. When he disclosed their family relationship they were rather taken aback. He asked one of his female colleagues what she thought of Ted and she replied, 'I'm about to get his autograph at our main broadcast studio. He's so incredible!' When Ashley told her that Ted was staying with us that week and actually using his bedroom, she genuinely could not believe it. It brought home to Ashley just how famous Ted had become in Australia, and the strong impression he had made.

After Ted left, Dad stayed on with us for a further three weeks. He enjoyed his visit immensely. We took him to Healsville Sanctuary to see the kangaroos there and he also accompanied me on several working visits to a few of my major customers. Australia, being a young country, had such a vastly different working environment compared to the familiar, carless Yorkshire of Dad's working life, in the years before and during the Second World War. From time to time Dad would comment on the lovely houses, but kept asking where all the factories were and where people worked. After seeing the GMH (General Motors Holden) factory at Fisherman's Bend and a few agricultural manufacturers, he at last said he understood that it was different from the working environment of Yorkshire, where rows of houses were built around and right up to the tall mills, the weaving sheds, the clothing factories, all within walking distance before cars came onto the scene.

Back in England, in 1976, following Jack Orchard's death earlier that year, Ted and Carol had sold their livestock. Ted wrote in November 1977:

> Sorry to be so long writing to you. Life has been very odd and confused lately. I'm going through a phase of feeling suffocated by the thousand daily

demands – not an hour without a phone call, every morning three or four letters from people all wanting something ... I feel like the bird that is perfectly free except for the tiny thread of nylon tying its leg to the post. But that's after a year of doing a great many readings – too many ... Dad's O.K. – but the time is rapidly approaching when he'll no longer be able to live alone. He's in good form, on the whole. Just more & more vague. Gets up at 7 in the evening sometimes. ... You should have come over & played at farming. Interesting life. I hate the feeling that certain dreams are fizzling out – in exchange for what?

Dad and me outside his cottage in North Tawton during our 1978 visit.

Our next trip to England was in 1978. What a memorable visit that was. We stayed at Court Green with Carol and Ted, and Dad joined us once again. This was to be the last time I saw him. I remember Dad challenging me to a game of snooker. I made it clear to him that I did not play, but he insisted on teaching me. One morning we drove to the Burton Hall hotel in North Tawton, which had a fully equipped billiards room. Here for the next three hours he defeated me in every game. He played like a pro! On returning to Ted, Carol and Joan at Court Green, he praised my attempts to Ted over a few ales, saying how well I'd played 'for a beginner'.

Snooker players in action - in Australia this time.

I remember also that on 27 July the renowned photographer Bill Brandt arrived at Court Green. He was commissioned to photograph Ted, who had agreed reluctantly, on condition that he could choose the image for publication. 'Of course,' said Brandt. Well, that didn't happen, did it, and Ted really disliked the one which is in circulation.

Over the ensuing years, Ted continued to write to us regularly, sending books and keeping us apprised of his literary activities, travels and, most importantly, the family. A chatty letter, sent in June 1979, brought us up to date: the weather was 'red hot', Nick had fallen off a bike at 30mph going downhill having hit a breeze block. When he picked him up from school, Ted found him 'black from brow to throat, with a snout like a wart-hog'. The other news was that Frieda was 'hurtling irresistibly and with increasing velocity towards marriage', that Olwyn had just married, Carol was well and the land was now worth £1,000–£1,500 an acre.

Later that year, Ted and Nicholas went to Iceland fishing and just managed to get back to Devon the day before Frieda's marriage. A year after that, Ted set off on a trip to Alaska with Nicholas, who had come to share his love of fishing and had obtained a place at Oxford to study zoology. Ted found Alaska 'fantastic', first of all participating in a literary conference in Fairbanks, before setting off on various expeditions, one by canoe (he was persuaded to take a rifle in case they encountered 'a nasty bear'). 'We got the lot,' wrote Ted. 'Wolves howling at night around the tent, near collision in the river with Moose.' Ted and Nick palled up with a fanatical angler, a Frenchman who worked as a guide in the autumn and was full of rich, entertaining stories. He led them to a place where they caught 'King Salmon'. Ted reported that he got two and Nick one. Ted was in his element. The rivers were teeming with the salmon, the beach was trampled with bear tracks and scattered with shed moose-horns, eagles floated above the giant mountains and the marvellous valleys were thick with flowers – 'acres of blue lupins' – and completely empty.

Sadly, our father had become very frail, as Ted described in a letter dated February 1981: 'Dad is now very low. My impression is he could die any minute, & no doubt suddenly will. I go every other day now, and each time his face seems even more changed – just a tiny ancient bird now, & obviously not happy.'

Dear old Dad passed away a few days later. Sadly, we were unable to come over for his funeral in Heptonstall, but we were comforted by the knowledge that not only were Ted and Carol there, but Olwyn, Frieda and Nicholas too, and my aunt Hilda. While the others threw freesias into the grave, Ted, fittingly, threw in a handful of 'wet, horrible, Heptonstall soil'.

Earlier I mentioned how Ted and I regretted that

Dad couldn't be drawn to talk about his war experiences in more depth. Ted movingly articulates this regret in his poem 'For the Duration', which I am glad to include here as a fitting tribute to a courageous and dearly loved man.

For the Duration

I felt a strange fear when the war-talk,
Like a creeping barrage, approached you.
Jig and jag I'd fitted much of it together.
Our treasure, your DCM – again and again
Carrying in the wounded
Collapsing with exhaustion. And as you collapsed
A shell-burst
Just in front of you lifting you upright
For the last somnambulist yards
Before you fell under your load into the trench.
The shell, some other time, that buried itself
Between your feet as you walked
And thoughtfully failed to go off.
The shrapnel hole, over your heart – how it spun you.
The blue scar of the bullet at your ankle
From a traversing machine-gun that tripped you
As you cleared the parapet. Meanwhile
The horrors were doled out, everybody
Had his appalling tale.
But what alarmed me most
Was your silence. Your refusal to tell.

I had to hear from others What you survived and
what you did.

Maybe you didn't want to frighten me.
Now it's too late.
Now I'd ask you shamelessly.
But then I felt ashamed.
What was my shame? Why couldn't I have borne
To hear you telling what you underwent?
Why was your war so much more unbearable
Than anybody else's? As if nobody else
Knew how to remember. After some uncle's
Virtuoso tale of survival
That made me marvel and laugh –
I looked at your face, your cigarette
Like a dial-finger. And my mind
Stopped with numbness.

Your day-silence was the coma
Out of which your night-dreams rose shouting.
I could hear you from my bedroom –
The whole hopelessness still going on,
No man's land still crying and burning
Inside our house, and you climbing again
Out of the trench, and wading back into the glare

As if you might still not manage to reach us
And carry us to safety.

In 1983, Ted was off to join Nicholas again, who was then on a research expedition to Kenya. Ted had expected to find Kenya menacing, but to his surprise felt wonderfully at ease and happy there. Nick, he told us, had spent two or three months 'cutting up and examining the stomachs of a thousand Nile fish'. Ted joined him on the southern tip of Rusinga Island, in the north-eastern part of Lake Victoria, where Nick was living with the headman of a small community of fishermen ('Eight mud huts,' wrote Ted). Ted was enthralled by the way they fished, pulling in between 150 and 300 fish a day in their nets and taking them by canoe to sell in the market. 'What biblical scenes,' exclaimed Ted. 'When I got there Nick was well installed and very popular ... I was stunned by the way Nicky handled them. Whatever he wanted done he got them to do – immediately. He is so purpose-ful.' Apart from enjoying the exciting fishing, Ted was clearly immensely proud of the important research Nick was doing.

It was heart-warming for us to see how close Ted's relationship with both Nicholas and Frieda had become. He was hugely admiring of their achieve-ments. In 1988 he wrote to say he was off to Alaska again for three weeks with Nicholas. 'We shall drift down a river from the big lake at the top – about a week or more. In the lake we shall try to take trout and Nicky's speciality, turbot ... finally we should come to

the battalions of the Kings – the big ones.' Ted was
looking forward to linking up with a friend of Nick's,
a bear biologist and a great character who, evidently,
had got a bear's skull for Ted's collection. He told me:
'Nicky scampers about that mighty wilderness like
a tireless little wolf. Writes his scientific papers. Has a
very high reputation among zoologists there.'

A very proud Ted with his giant Nile perch, 1983.

In October Ted wrote to let us know that Frieda was
coming to Australia. He seemed to have a feeling she
might decide to live there and indeed she moved to

Perth in 1991. Ted was very proud of Frieda's many talents, her poetry, her painting, her sculpture, and sang her praises. He told us she'd sculpted some faces in relief, the psychological detail of which he found 'uncanny'. In her paintings, he continued, 'that psychological knowledge is truly supreme. Everything about her paintings is magical.' She was also, it seemed, a phenomenal dressmaker.

Frieda, said Ted, would amuse us; she was 'full of go' – and so we found her. She visited us on a number of occasions, although she was based in Perth in Western Australia, while we live about an hour and a half from Melbourne. Frieda had grown into an attractive, intelligent young lady, highly motivated with a good business head, and was deeply committed to her painting, sketching and writing. She brought some fine work with her that she planned to exhibit in Melbourne, which impressed us greatly.

Frieda loved our seaside environment, and we spent many happy hours exchanging stories, learning about her inspiring projects and reminiscing. She also enjoyed meeting up with Ashley and Brendon – both now grown up, of course. The boys had started their own neighbourhood band in the early 1970s, practising constantly. Ashley was the lead singer/guitarist and Brendon was an impressive drummer. Later, Ashley kept up his creative urges as a songwriter and performed some of his original compositions around

Melbourne and the surrounding country towns. Frieda showed great interest in his music and during her visits to the city they talked about his experiences of playing in the band, songwriting and working for ABC.

Chapter Twelve

Poet Laureate

In November 1984 Ted and Carol went on a cruise up the Nile with their friends the writer Michael Morpurgo and his wife Clare. In the mountain of mail awaiting Ted on their return was a letter from 10 Downing Street inviting him to take on the office of Poet Laureate, which he was honoured to accept. The announcement was made on 19 December.

In a letter to me the following June, Ted wrote wittily about the 'job':

> The last few months have been quite curious – getting used to being reported by everybody as a superior kind of freak. The 60 million who would never know the difference between what I write & 3 blind mice are ready to extend me every possible kind of credit. So it becomes quite a problem – not to blow it. It actually means I have to be quite careful – what I get involved in etc. Mainly, people want to involve me in their enterprises – as a sort of dayglo publicity

substance, painted over their whole image. So much of my life is an elaboration of all the possible polite ways of saying no. But even that little involvement means I'm made aware of infinite numbers of people fixing me with a beady eye wondering how they can turn me to their advantage. Odd business. I'm not sure I've solved it yet.

In the autumn of 1986 Ted and Carol were invited by the Sherry Institute to Jerez for Ted to taste and select his Laureate 'sack'. Ted told me that in actuality the sherry didn't arrive for another four or five years!

Ted signing his butt of sack in the Bodega, Jerez, 1986.

Then, in 1990, Ted invited Joan and me to join him and some friends – all dedicated fishermen – for a fishing trip on the river Tay in Scotland. We had, in

fact, already planned a trip to the UK, so we gladly accepted the offer. As it happened, the trip coincided with Ted receiving an honorary DLitt at the University of Aberdeen. Arriving in London, we hired a car and travelled to Scotland, passing through Lockerbie near the scene of the terrible airliner disaster, and joining up with Ted and Carol at an amazing hotel called the Kinnaird for lunch. It was an emotional and truly happy reunion. The following week was a great success, although with very few salmon caught – apparently it was a bad year for them. But we enjoyed meeting Ted's friends immensely. I didn't catch a single fish, but I did a lot of sketching of the beautiful countryside.

Ted writing and me sketching in Devon, summer 1990.

Unfortunately, halfway through the week Joan pulled a back muscle and Ted and I carried her to the car, then into Perth to a doctor, after which she was obliged to relax and read for the remaining days of our trip. We took a room in a charming small hotel, which had recently opened. The good food and the owner's cheerful hospitality made it a real home from home. Ted was so impressed he promptly booked a room and joined us.

Ted's fishing friends arranged a final splendid dinner for us and then Ted went to Sheffield to receive another DLitt, taking with him our aunt Hilda. He then drove back to Devon with her, in preparation for our visit, and we joined them there on 15 July.

Ted seemed really pleased that we were going to spend more time together. But even our presence could not distract him from his work. He was constantly making notes for future poems. I never saw him without a notebook protruding from his pocket; he said that he regarded it as part of himself. As Poet Laureate, he was writing a poem for the Queen Mother's ninetieth birthday, which was then less than a month away. Joan and I contributed by adding a missing punctuation mark!

During our stay Ted and I visited several of his favourite fishing spots in Devon. Throughout his years at Court Green Ted fished for trout and salmon in the Taw and in the Torridge from 1976. He really was a

fine fisherman and more successful than me. Those were precious days and, as it transpired, it was the final fishing we were ever to enjoy together. There was an enormous amount of socialising and jolly eating and drinking at Court Green, down at the riverside, and in local hostelries. And every evening at Court Green, led by Aunt Hilda, the 'sundowners' would be sipped and glugged on the lawn – what a time we had.

When we got back to Australia we received a letter from Ted that I found poignant then and even more so now. Looking back on our visit, he seemed to feel that we had left just when we had got to the point, as he put it, where we should have been beginning our stay. He felt he had organised too much for us when we could have simply lounged about together chatting, and that there were always other people around 'sitting on our arms and shoulders like a lot of parrots'. The evenings at the river were good, he said, but not long enough, and there were too many distractions. He declared that he was very surprised at himself and how long it took him to come into focus. 'But just those last few days,' he continued, 'I could feel myself coming back to where we left off. But I think you too, Gerald, took time to readjust – the same.'

It had, indeed, been a long time since our previous visit and being together again had made him wish we were nearer – and naturally I shared those sentiments. 'If you were,' he concluded, 'I'm sure my life wouldn't be half so silly.' One thing cheered him, an 'amazing' letter from the Queen Mother, evidently responding to the poem he had written for her. Ted had first met the Queen Mother in the summer of 1987 and since then he and Carol had stayed several times at Royal Lodge in Windsor Great Park. Clearly, they had become friendly, and Ted also always enjoyed staying as the Queen Mother's guest at Birkhall on the Balmoral Estate and fishing there. 'Funny old corner I've got myself into,' said Ted, before reverting to his opening theme. 'I so wish you were just arriving so we could have the time all over again – so I could treat it properly and really wake up to it.'

In December that year Ted let us know that he had been diagnosed with shingles. He was staying up very late working on his Shakespeare *magnum opus* and this obviously took its toll. The fact that the shingles affected his eyesight was a curiosity to him because of the people he was writing about at the time, especially King Lear. It took him almost three months to recover.

In 1993 he wrote to describe a visit to Canada during which he'd taken part in a fundraising dinner and, of course, seized the opportunity to fish in the Pacific, with porpoises 'doing their silent, slow motion stunts all around us'. Back in England, Ted wrote enthusiastically about Frieda's painting, telling us that she'd completed all the pieces for her exhibition. He found that some of her latest work had 'a kind of dazzling beauty – fairly takes your breath away'. He and Carol, he said, were going to buy one – of an orange Christmas tree. Olwyn, he reported, had given up her literary agency and, as Ted put it, had thereby 'freed herself from the world of Plath'. Ted himself, of course – as we saw when he came to Australia – continued to be hounded by biographers of Sylvia. At one point, he told us, four books were being written in the US, and one young American English teacher had 'walked into a US publisher, announced his plans of writing another Plath biography, and walked out with a $140,000 advance'. Naturally, every biographer had to try to find a new sensational angle.

Ted was diagnosed with cancer in April 1997 and word soon reached us. He had surgery and treatment, to which he responded very well. That summer he took various fishing trips, and in September he and Carol sold Moortown. In November of that year the artist Leonard Baskin, with whom Ted had collaborated over the years, came with his wife Lisa from the States, and they visited again the following spring. I recently came across a photo, taken that spring, of Ted with Leonard among the daffodils outside Ted's writing hut in the garden. The daffodils remind me that in their days at Court Green, Ted and Sylvia, being very short of money, would sell daffodils to the locals – a tradition of the house.

The publication of Ted's *Birthday Letters* in January 1998 was an enormous release for him, and the reception the book received was incredible. I knew what a hard and painful book it was for him to write and I felt enormously pleased for him. I also felt particularly proud when I heard that his *Tales from Ovid*, published the previous year, was the Whitbread Book of the Year.

For all his fishing experience, one kind of fishing Ted had never done was called 'bonefishing'. But in March he and Carol were invited to do just that off the coast of Cuba. Bonefish (*Albula vulpes*) are considered to be a worthy challenge for any keen angler, and bonefishing is a thrilling, shallow-water pursuit played out in water ranging from eight inches to several feet in depth. What a trip. Ted's account made me quite envious.

Ted's very positive attitude to his illness was revealed in a letter he sent me in April 1998 – a letter he'd written to assuage our worries. He'd tried not to broadcast his illness, saying that his instinct about letting people know you're ill was 'like the antelope's instinct that doesn't want the leopards and hyenas to notice its limp'. He felt that every person who believed he was ill was an obstacle to his getting better. He went on to say that his doctors said he was 'safe', that he was in good spirits and wasn't really aware that he was ill. 'So, nearest and dearest, don't let that steam come screaming out of your ears.' He promised, 'If I suddenly get really ill, don't worry, I'll tell you.'

He ended the letter on a positive note, telling us that the garden was lovely, that *Birthday Letters* continued to sit on the bestseller list on both sides of the Atlantic, that he had a big theatrical production coming up in August with Diana Rigg – his translation of Racine's *Phèdre* – and then, at the end of the year, at the National, his translation of *The Oresteia*. 'I am writing away,' he concluded.

In August the announcement was made that Ted was to receive the Order of Merit. It was presented to him by the Queen on 16 October at Buckingham Palace, an occasion he described in cheerful detail in a letter to Aunt Hilda soon afterwards, and also in a phone call to me. 'Wouldn't it have pleased Ma,' he wrote to Hilda. Ted had given the Queen a copy of *Birthday Letters* and told her how he'd come to write and publish it. 'I suppose, talking about those poems, I was able to open my heart more than ever before – and so she responded in kind.'

Sadly however, as we feared, Ted's cancer began to overwhelm him, and on 20 October he phoned me to say that he was going into hospital for surgery. We talked of the old days and the precious time we had

had as brothers. He described the Order of Merit medal in greater detail, how proud and honoured he felt in receiving it from the Queen, and how he'd like to show it to me. We conversed for an hour. It was 3 a.m. our time and Joan got out of bed to join in the conversation. Finally, he said, 'I'll let you know how I go.'

In that conversation I was able to tell Ted just how proud I was of him and all he had achieved. They were to be the last words I ever spoke to him. Ted died on 28 October. Olwyn, Carol, Frieda and Nicholas, who had arrived that morning from Alaska, were all at his bedside.

And so our last, and saddest, trip to England was to attend Ted's memorial service, held in Westminster Abbey on 13 May 1999 – by coincidence the thirtieth anniversary of our mother's death. What a moving and awe-inspiring occasion that was, what an honour for Ted – but then he had been Poet Laureate for fourteen years – and what a journey from humble beginnings back in Mytholmroyd, all those years ago. Present at the ceremony were His Royal Highness The Prince of Wales and Her Majesty Queen Elizabeth The Queen Mother – Prince Charles showing touching concern for his grandmother – representatives of The Queen and Prince Philip, Princess Margaret and Princess Anne, and of course his family, as well as many poets, friends and admirers of Ted's work.

WESTMINSTER ABBEY

Service of Thanksgiving
for the
Life and Work of
TED HUGHES, OM, OBE
1930 – 1998
Poet Laureate

Thursday 13 May 1999
11.00 am

The cover of the order of service.

The service was conducted by the Dean of Westminster. Carol had invited the Tallis Scholars, whose choral singing Ted had grown fond of. And how beautiful their singing was. Among those who spoke, read poems and paid tribute to Ted were Lord Gowrie, Dr Caroline Tisdall, the poet Michael Baldwin and Ted's great friend Seamus Heaney, the Nobel Laureate, who called Ted 'a guardian spirit of the land and language'. Referring obliquely to the tragedies that had stalked Ted's life, Heaney said, 'The learning in his art was marked by personal and stoic sorrow', as indeed it was. Reflecting Ted's deep love of Beethoven, the service also included the adagio from Beethoven's

Sonata No. 17 in D, played by the great pianist Alfred Brendel, whom Ted admired hugely, and concluded, fittingly, with a recording of Ted himself reading Shakespeare's song from *Cymbeline*. Ted's voice resonating through the abbey was a haunting moment nobody who was present will ever forget.

Our visit to England lasted nearly three weeks. We made a brief trip to Yorkshire, spent a few days in London before the service, and passed the rest of the time in Devon at Court Green with Carol and members of the family, meeting some of Ted and Carol's friends. Then, sadly, we bade our farewells and reluctantly returned home.

In the years since Ted's death it had been suggested that he should be memorialised in Poet's Corner in Westminster Abbey, where Chaucer, Spenser, Dryden, Tennyson and Browning are buried and a very select group of great English poets from over the centuries commemorated, among them Milton, Wordsworth, Keats, Shelley, Byron and Blake. When I learnt that this was finally going to happen I was enormously proud that Ted should receive this fantastic accolade, and only sorry that Joan and I were unable to be present, since unfortunately periods of ill health now prevented us from undertaking such a long journey. Carol and Frieda were there, of course, and we had to content ourselves with the photographs Carol sent us, the reports in the press ... and the memories.

The dedication of the ledger took place on the evening of 6 December 2011. Unveiled by Seamus Heaney, the stone sits at the foot of the memorial for T. S. Eliot, who died in 1965. This seemed such an appropriate place, given Ted's enormous admiration and respect for T. S. Eliot, which he described in his diary upon hearing of Eliot's death. I can do no better than quote Ted's moving words:

> ... like a crack over the head, exactly, followed by headache. Heavy after-effects. I've so tangled him into my thoughts, as the guru-in-chief, and dreamed of him so clearly and unambiguously that this will have consequences for me. At once I felt windswept, unsafe. At the same time, realised that from now on everything will be different. He was in my mind constantly, like a rather ever-watchful, ever-powerful father, and now he has gone, I shall have to move – be able to move, maybe.
>
> His being my publisher simply sealed his paternity. How often I've thought of going to ask for his blessing.

The lines below, which appear on Ted's ledger stone, and with which I end this personal memoir and journey, are from Ted's poem 'That Morning'. They describe a fishing experience he'd shared with his son Nicholas, thus embracing his memory too:

> So we found the end of our journey.

> So we stood, alive in the river of light
> Among the creatures of light, creatures of light.
> *Ted Hughes OM*
> 1930–1998

THOMAS
STEARNS
ELIOT
O M

BORN 26 SEPTEMBER 1888
DIED 4 JANUARY 1965

'the communication
the dead is tongued with fire beyond
the language of the living'

'the creatures of light.' ... 'So we found the end of our journey. So we stood, alive in the river of light Among the creatures of light.'

TED
HUGHES
O M
1930·1998

Notebook

Since some of Ted's poems are so clearly rooted in the area and places we frequented in our shared childhood days, I thought it might be helpful – by way of a flashback – to pinpoint just a few of the more famous ones. The page numbers refer to his *Collected Poems*, published by Faber and Faber in 2003.

'The Horses' p. 22
Set in the moors above Mytholmroyd, Yorkshire.

'Crow Hill' p. 62
Set around farms above Mytholmroyd, Yorkshire.

'Hawk Roosting' p. 68
Ted and I used to roam Redacre Woods in Mytholmroyd, Yorkshire as boys.

'The Retired Colonel' p. 77
This colonel lived in North Tawton, Devon, just up the road from Court Green. I never met this character;

he died some years ago. Ted and Sylvia knew him well, though.

'Pike' p. 84
Ted and I fished this pond – at an old estate near home – in 1938–39 and 1946.

'Sunstroke' p. 86
Set at Old Denaby, near Mexborough, Yorkshire. I was in the RAF at the time (1940–44); Ted was attending Mexborough Grammar School, where he won a state scholarship to Cambridge University.

'Her Husband' p. 148
This couple lived next to Dad's newsagents shop at 75 Main Street, Mexborough, Yorkshire. The husband worked at the large Denaby coal pit and behaved exactly as Ted says here.

'Out' p. 165
Set at 1 Aspinall Street, Banksfields, Mytholmroyd, Yorkshire, where Ted and I went to council school. We moved to Mexborough when Ted was about eight years old, in 1938.

'Heptonstall' p. 492
Heptonstall churchyard, where both my parents lie. Sylvia Plath is also buried nearby.

Picture Credits

Copyright and by kind permission of the Estate of Ted Hughes, pp. 1, 111, 129, 132, 135, 142, 143, 152, 159, 200, 201; plate section one pp. 2 (top left, bottom right), 3, 6 (top left, bottom left, bottom right), 7, 8 (top); plate section two pp. 1, 2, 3 (bottom left, bottom middle), 4, 5 (bottom), 6, 7 (bottom)

Copyright and by kind permission of the Estate of Nicholas Hughes, p. 195; plate section two p. 3 (top)

Copyright and by kind permission of Carol Hughes, pp. 178, 209, 213; plate section one p. 8 (bottom); plate section two pp. 3 (bottom right), 5 (top), 7 (top, middle)

Copyright Paloma Mattin, reproduced by kind permission of Carol Hughes, p.175

Copyright and by kind permission of Lady Penn, plate section two p. 8 (middle)

All other photos and sketches the property of the author